JESUS CHRIST

THE

MASTER EVANGELIST

HOW TO PRESENT THE GOSPEL
THE WAY JESUS DID

By
Philip DelRe

Jesus Christ
The Master Evangelist
Philip DelRe

INTRODUCTION

When it comes to proving the existence of God, and the reality of heaven and hell, Jesus said:

> If they won't believe Moses, neither would they believe
> if someone they knew came back from the dead to warn
> them of the judgment to come. Luke 16:19-31

According to the Bible, there is a real Person called God, a real person called Satan, a real place called heaven, and a real place called hell. According to Jesus, there is one thing (associated with Moses), that represents a more compelling argument for their existence, than someone you know coming back from the dead to warn you of the judgment to come!

That one thing is what this book is all about. When it comes to evangelism, there is one universal truth that has more power to change lives than all the scientific, philosophical, and legal arguments combined. This fact represents the church's most powerful apologetic weapon.

When it comes to sharing our faith, God did not leave us to fend for ourselves. The Bible reveals a perfect, systematic theology of evangelism that cannot be improved upon by any man. Just as mathematics is a perfect science, so is presenting the gospel.

Join me as we sit at the feet of Jesus Christ, the Master Evangelist, to discover the most powerful, most life changing truth in the most powerful, life changing book ever written—the Bible!

ACKNOWLEDGMENTS

Giving all honor, glory, and praise to God, for the Spirit of wisdom and revelation, without which it is impossible to correctly interpret His word. Thank you also, Lord, for my wife, Susan, who believed in me when I didn't. I would also like to acknowledge Walter Chantry, and Ray Comfort. These are the men God used to teach me how to present the best news anyone could ever hear, *in context*. And, to our faithful partners who helped make all this possible, we love you.

Praise the Lord!

TABLE OF CONTENTS

CHAPTER ONE

THE
MOST AWESOME
DISPLAY OF POWER
THE WORLD HAS EVER SEEN

In northwestern Saudi Arabia, out in the middle of the desert, and surrounded by oceans of sand, there is a small "top secret" military outpost. A handful of Saudi marksmen armed with automatic weapons and guard dogs patrol an area surrounded by a chain-link fence. Their mission? To keep any and all curiosity seekers away from this site. In addition to the military patrol (remember this is in the middle of nowhere), there is a large sign posted in front of the guard house, outside the fence, carrying this warning in Arabic and in English:

> This is a protected archeological site
> All trespassers will be prosecuted

So, what's behind the fence that the Saudi government does not want the world to see? Shrouded in secrecy, is an 8,465 foot mountain known to the local Bedouins as Jabal Musa. You can find it on a good map under the name Jabal Al Lawz. So, why would anyone want to "protect" a mountain out in the middle of the desert? If the facts about this mountain were made public, and if the Saudis allowed people to examine this area, Biblical scholars, archeologists, and journalists would hail this as one of, if not the greatest, archeological discovery of all time! The effect, however, would be a disaster for the Saudis and Islam. What happened here is so significant, and the evidence is so overwhelmingly conclusive, if word got out, there are many people from all over the world who would be willing to risk their lives by sneaking into the country to see this incredible sight. Some already have, *that* is why the area is guarded. Since the Saudi's preferred method of dealing with "infidels" [non- Muslims] is beheading, the potential to create *another* international crisis similar to the fight for control over the Temple Mount in Jerusalem is real!

1

WHAT IS SO UNUSUAL ABOUT
THIS MOUNTAIN?

At the base of the mountain there is a huge formation of boulders (some weighing hundreds of tons) carefully placed on top of one another, three stories high, a hundred feet across, and flat on top. This engineering feat required either a crane, or a large number of people who were *highly motivated,* and with a good deal of experience moving stones of this magnitude without the aid of modern technology. Whoever it was that went to all this trouble also had a fetish for cattle. Etched into the sides of this giant memorial are pictures of cows and bulls. Strange indeed, since cattle are not indigenousness to the desert. In addition, there are large piles of smaller rocks every four hundred yards forming a semicircle around the mountain. They appear to serve as boundary markers, as if to say, "This far and no farther." At the foot of the mountain there is a v-shaped pit, with carefully placed stones along the sides to form walls. Next to that, there are 12 hand hewn pillars made of stone, which represent a memorial to something very significant to someone. The question is, who?

Most unusual of all is the fact that the mountain itself (made of solid granite rock) is brown, but the peek (the top third of the mountain) is shiny black. It appears as if the top of the mountain had been exposed to an intense heat and melted by a giant incinerator!

Scholars and archeologists who have examined the sum of evidence on and around this mountain (based on eye witness accounts, pictures, and video tape smuggled out of the country), are convinced that this is the actual site where God gave Moses the Ten Commandments! All of the evidence matches perfectly with the Biblical account of the Israelites' Exodus from Egypt. The New Testament affirms that Mt. Sinai is in Arabia (see Gal. 4:25).

Providentially, it only rains a fraction of an inch every ten years in this area, so the effects left by God, and 2-3 million Israelites, have been well preserved for thousands of years. There are a number of great books and videos documenting the facts of this discovery that are nothing short of spectacular![1]

SO, WHAT DOES ALL THIS HAVE TO DO
WITH YOU?
EVERYTHING. KEEP READING!

One question people often ask is, "How did we get the Bible?" In 2 Peter 1:21 we are told: "For no prophecy was ever made by an act of human will, but men moved by the Holy Spirit spoke from God." However, there is one part of the Bible that stands alone. Exodus 31:18 tells us that God wrote the Ten Commandments *with His own finger!*

> And when He had finished speaking with him upon Mount Sinai, He gave Moses the two tablets of the testimony, tablets of stone, written by the finger of God.

It is impossible to overstate the theological and the practical significance of this fact. Accordingly, God's emphasis on the moral law does not end there, it begins there. The revelation at Mt. Sinai also represents the one and only time (from Genesis to Revelation) that God descended to earth in His omnipotent state, and spoke audibly to the *entire* nation of Israel!

THE GREATEST SERMON EVER PREACHED

While there are many miracles recorded in scripture, three are in a class by themselves. Only creation (which no human witnessed), and the resurrection of Jesus Christ compare in terms of power, glory, and significance to what happened at Mt. Sinai. Herbert Lockyer, in his book, *All the Miracles of the Bible*, agrees. Speaking of the revelation at Sinai, he said there has never been "So awful a manifestation...at any other place or time, nor will be until the end time period of human history."[2]

God's message from Mt. Sinai was accompanied by an entourage of sight and sound so dreadful, so terrifying, that when it was over, the people begged Moses never to let God speak to them directly again. They were convinced that one more manifestation of that magnitude would literally kill them (Ex. 20:19). This raises a most important and fundamental question. Why would God do such a thing to His own people? What was the point in almost scaring them to death?

3

I would like *you* to discover the answer by reading an abbreviated version of the Biblical account yourself.

> The LORD also said to Moses, "For on the third day the LORD will come down on Mount Sinai in the sight of all the people. And you shall set bounds for the people all around, saying,
>
> 'Beware that you do not go up on the mountain or touch the border of it; whoever touches the mountain shall surely be put to death. No hand shall touch him, but he shall surely be stoned or shot through; whether beast or man, he shall not live.
>
> 'When the ram's horn sounds a long blast, they shall come up to the mountain.'"
>
> So it came about on the third day, when it was morning, that there were thunder and lightning flashes and a thick cloud upon the mountain and a very loud trumpet sound, so that all the people who were in the camp trembled.
>
> And Moses brought the people out of the camp to meet God, and they stood at the foot of the mountain. Now Mount Sinai was all in smoke because the LORD descended upon it in fire; and its smoke ascended like the smoke of a furnace, and the whole mountain quaked violently.
>
> When the sound of the trumpet grew louder and louder, Moses spoke and God answered him with thunder. And the LORD came down on Mount Sinai, to the top of the mountain.
>
> Then God spoke all these words, saying, "I am the LORD your God, who brought you out of the land of Egypt, out of the house of slavery. Thou shalt have no other gods before Me.
>
> Thou shalt not make for yourself an idol.

4

Thou shalt not take the name of the LORD your God in vain.

Remember the Sabbath day, to keep it holy.

Honor your father and your mother.

Thou shalt not murder.

Thou shalt not commit adultery.

Thou shalt not steal.

Thou shalt not lie.

Thou shalt not covet against thy neighbor."

And all the people perceived the thunder and the lightning flashes and the sound of the trumpet and the mountain smoking; and when the people saw it, they trembled and stood at a distance.

Then they said to Moses, "Speak to us yourself and we will listen; but let not God speak to us, lest we die."

And Moses said to the people, "Do not be afraid; for God has come in order to test you, and in order that the fear of Him may remain with you, so that you may not sin." (Ex. 20:1-20)

The question before us is, why would God almost scare His own people to death? ". . . In order that the fear of God would remain with the people, *so that they may not sin!*"

Obviously, God is trying to make a point that none of us will ever forget. The benefits of understanding the doctrine of sin, and conversely, the doctrine of holiness, are foundational to not only understanding the Bible, but also in developing an intimate and personal relationship with God. It is sin after all that separates us from God. This is what the Lord Himself said through the prophet Isaiah:

> But your iniquities have made a separation between
> you and your God, and your sins have hidden His face
> from you, so that He does not hear. Isa. 59:2

There is another benefit to having a clear understanding of the doctrine of sin, and that has to do with our God-given privilege and responsibility of communicating the gospel to a lost and dying world. Sin is what Jesus came to save us from.

> And she will bear a Son; and you shall call His name
> Jesus, for it is He who will save His people from their
> sins. Matt. 1:21

"There is no fact as evident and no subject so important as that of sin . . . a right concept of sin is therefore imperative for if man errs here, he errs everywhere."[3]

"Initially we fear looking squarely at our sins, lest we get overwhelmed. But the reverse turns out to be true. The more we see the depth of our sin, the more we realize the height of God's love."[4]

KEEP READING!

SMALL GROUP DISCUSSION
QUESTIONS FOR CHAPTER ONE.

1. Read Romans 3:11-18. How are the unsaved characterized?

2. In terms of how the Bible was written (see 2 Pet. 1:21), how are the Ten Commandments different?

3. How is that significant?

4. What does "etched in stone" symbolize?

5. List each commandment one at a time and answer the question: What would happen to our world if everyone obeyed this commandment?

6. Was the Law given before or after the Israelites were redeemed from Egyptian slavery? How is that significant?

7. How can the fear of God be positive?

8. What did you learn from this chapter?

9. Memorize the Ten Commandments for next week.

10. According to statistics 95% of people who call themselves Christians have never even attempted to lead another person to Christ, and 70% of them think it is wrong to interfere with another person's belief system. What does that say about the church?

CHAPTER TWO

SOMETHING OLD SOMETHING NEW
SOMETHING BOLD SOMETHING TRUE

Understanding the relationship that exists between the Old and the New Testaments will add light-years to your understanding of the Bible.

The Old Testament is commonly referred to as "The Law," and the New Testament is known conceptually as "The Gospel of grace." To be sure, grace is found in the Old Testament (Gen. 15:6 for example), and Law in the New (I will show you that in a moment). But, the predominant themes respectively are: Law in the Old, grace in the New; in that order and for good reason. Simply stated, it is because we have broken God's Law that we need His grace (i.e., mercy). Grace presupposes Law. The importance of understanding these two foundational Biblical principles, and their relationship to each other, *cannot be overstated.*

Without the New Testament, the Old Testament would be incomplete, and without the Old Testament, the New Testament would be utterly incomprehensible. Each is a guide to properly understanding the other. The Old Testament is the foundation upon which the New Testament is built, and the New Testament constantly refers back to the Old to establish its validity. Through fulfilled prophecy, each continuously points back and forth to the other as proof positive of its divine authenticity and its perfect unity.

The very first verse in the New Testament forces you to this inescapable conclusion.

> This is the record of the genealogy of Jesus Christ the
> Son of David, the Son of Abraham. Matt. 1:1

Without understanding the covenant promises that God made with Abraham and David, Matt. 1:1 would be utterly boring. Yet, to those who understand it in the context of the Old Testament, this verse explodes with excitement! Matthew 1:1 shows us two things. First, that God always keeps His promises, and secondly, that the Bible is one book! It says in effect, *If you are starting here, you have to go back to Genesis man!* Who would pick up any other book and start reading right in the middle? Yet, people do that with the Bible, and wonder why they have trouble understanding it. "Starting in Matthew is like walking into a movie half-way through. It's like thinking you are telling a good joke when all you can remember is the punch line!"[1]

The Old Testament contains truths that are essential for a proper worldview that are found in no other source. For example, only in the book of Genesis (which means origin) do we discover the origin of the universe, of man and his fall into sin, the doctrine of marriage and the family, the establishment of the nations, languages, and the prophetic significance of Israel. The Old Testament reveals the rebellion in heaven, that turned Lucifer into Satan, and thus the origin of evil, and the promise of a Savior.

"The Old Testament worldview is clearly distinct from other worldviews, such as polytheism, pantheism, gnosticism, deism, atheism, and naturalism. The New Testament does not provide another worldview but simply assumes the one taught in the Old Testament."[2]

Most of us think of Matthew as the first book of the New Testament, and it is. In the English translation, Matthew is *also* the 40th book of the 66 that make up the Bible. The number 40 is significant, since throughout scripture it represents the number of completion.

According to Malachi 3:6, the Lord does not change. For God to change, He would either have to get better or worse, and that is impossible; He is perfect! Likewise, according to the New Testament (written 1500 years after Mt. Sinai) God's definition of *sin* has never changed either. 1 John 3:4 says,

> Whosoever commits sin transgresses the law: for sin is
> the transgression of the law. KJV

What Law is John referring to? The answer is found in the book written by the "Apostle to the Gentiles" to the *Christians* at Rome. Since Romans was written *after* the church age began (in Acts chapter two), and since it was written to Gentiles as well as to Jews, no one can claim we are teaching from the dispensation of the Old Testament. Isn't God good?

The book of Romans is considered by theologians to be the greatest treatise on the doctrine of *salvation by grace* in all of scripture. Martin Luther's commentary on the book begins with these words:

> This epistle is really the chief part of the New Testament and the very purest Gospel.

So, what does the chief part of the New Testament and the very purest gospel have to say about the Law? Much indeed. Beginning in Rom. 3:20 we read...

> because by the works of the Law no flesh will be justified in His sight; for through the Law {comes} the knowledge of sin.
>
> Do we then nullify the Law through faith? May it never be! On the contrary, we establish the Law. Rom. 3:31
>
> What shall we say then? Is the Law sin? May it never be! On the contrary, I would not have come to know sin except through the Law; for I would not have known about coveting if the Law had not said, "You shall not covet." Rom. 7:7

Romans 7:7 leaves no doubt, Paul is referring to the moral Law as contained in the Ten Commandments. What other Law would fit the context? With this understanding, we can *paraphrase* Romans 3:20 this way: "For by the works of the Law no flesh will be justified in His sight; for *through the Ten Commandments* comes the knowledge of sin."

Romans 3:31 proves beyond the shadow of a doubt that the moral Law has *not* been abolished by the coming of Christ. And, Romans 7:7 shows us that sin is still defined (not by the letter, but by the spirit) of the Ten Commandments (Matt. 5:21-28).

The ability to define sin is the ability to define exactly why a person needs Jesus Christ. Rather than telling a person he is a sinner, try defining sin for him, and watch the Holy Spirit do what only He can!

In 1855, Charles Haddon Spurgeon, one of the finest minds in the history of the church said this: "There is no point upon which men make greater mistakes, than upon the relation that exists between the law and the Gospel."

MANY PEOPLE EQUATE LAW WITH LEGALISM, AND SEE GRACE AS A WILDCARD YOU CAN PLAY ANYTIME YOU DON'T LIKE THE RULES!

Even though the Old Testament comprises 70% of the Bible, the word "Law" actually appears more times in the New Testament than in the Old. God is trying to tell us something. Meanwhile, Satan's campaign to distort the *legitimate* use of the Law (to define sin) has been so successful, that many Christian leaders and their congregations are scared to death of the word. The fear of being labeled a "legalist" is a powerful weapon in the hands of the enemy. Christian leaders can talk about holiness and obedience, as long as they do not use the word "law." One wonders what it is we are supposed to obey, and what constitutes holiness? Part of the reason for all the confusion is because the New Testament "appears" to contradict itself on this issue (see appendix one). The confusion is easily cleared up when we pay close attention to context.

Altogether, there are 613 laws that constitute Old Testament Judaism. Under this system, there was no so-called notion of "separation between church and state." That is, there was no distinction between secular and sacred law. To clarify our understanding of how the Law applies to the church, we must define our terms. While there is some overlap, there remains a distinction between the civil, the ceremonial, and the moral Law.

a. The civil law, such as not driving your chariot over 35 mph through Jerusalem on the Sabbath when children are present.

b. The ceremonial Law, which had to do with the Jewish religion of feasts, fasts, and the sacrificial system.

c. And, the moral Law, as contained in the Ten Commandments.

The civil law has no application for the 21st century Christians, since we are not citizens living under the government of ancient Israel. The ceremonial Laws (which included the sacrificing of animals) were prophetic road-signs pointing us to Christ. They were "fulfilled" legally, prophetically, spiritually, and literally when Jesus Christ, the sinless Lamb of God, was sacrificed, "once *and* for all" (Heb. 7:27;

9:12, 1 Pet. 3:18). As a result, we are no longer living under the dispensation of the Old Testament sacrificial system. However, the *definition* of sin (something God is still opposed to) has never changed. Remember, it is the New Testament that says, "... sin is (not was) the transgression of the Law."

So, how is it that we have come so far in losing the proper concept of the Law? Here is how it was done. Since we are saved by grace alone, and since the New Testament says, "Christ fulfilled the Law," sometime around the turn of the twentieth century, liberal "theologians" began to equate all "Law" with legalism. Legalism is the idea that you can add anything to or subtract anything from your salvation by what you do or don't do. The minute you add anything to grace, it is no longer grace. Legalism is heresy, heresy is false doctrine, and false doctrine is the work of the enemy.

The result of this misunderstanding leaves Christ between two thieves—antinomianism on one side (the idea that there is no law whatsoever in the New Testament) and legalism on the other. Both are equally deadly, and both are prevalent to one degree or another in the church.

THE LAW OF LOVE

One of the most strategic pieces of spiritual real estate temporarily controlled by the enemy is the idea that Law and love are opposing forces. Since love is the greatest gift, and God Himself is love, and since love endures forever, no one would dare be opposed to love. Therefore, whatever opposes love must be evil and done away with. Unfortunately, this is how the Law is perceived by many people. This understanding is completely erroneous.

The Ten Commandments are divided into two "tables." The first four are vertical, and teach us how to love God. The next six are horizontal, and teach us how to love our fellow man. Here is how Jesus summarized the Law:

> "Teacher, which is the greatest commandment in the *Law?*" Jesus replied: "Love the Lord your God with all your heart and with all your soul and with all your mind.' This is the first and greatest commandment.

> And the second is like it: 'Love your neighbor as your-self.' All the Law and the Prophets hang on these two commandments." Matthew 22:36–40

Here, Jesus Christ uses the words *Law* and *love* in the same breath! Rather than being mutually exclusive, Law and love are mutually affinitive. The Law shows me how to express my love for God and for my neighbor in a tangible way. See for yourself:

> Owe nothing to anyone except to love one another; for he who loves his neighbor has fulfilled {the} Law. For this, "You shall not commit adultery, you shall not murder, you shall not steal, you shall not covet," and if there is any other commandment, it is summed up in this saying, "you shall love your neighbor as your-self." Love does no wrong to a neighbor; love therefore is the fulfillment of {the} Law. Romans 13:8–10

Thanks to the moral Law, *love* can actually be weighed and measured against an objective standard. Without the guidelines of the Law, love would be abstract and relative. In 1 Cor. 13, we see the effects of love, whereas the moral Law defines its boundaries.

In His infinite wisdom, God tells us that "love is the fulfillment of the Law" (Rom. 13:10b). If I truly love my neighbor, according to Romans 13, I will honor his marriage covenant, and mine, by not lusting after his wife, I will forgive him when he wrongs me, rather than commit-ting murder, I will honor his property by not stealing it, I will tell him the truth (and what truth is) when I speak to him, and I will rejoice in the blessings God has given him, rather than coveting his goods. Isn't that the kind of neighborhood in which you would want to live? Can you even begin to imagine what would happen to our world if we all "kept the Law" according to this standard? Proverbs 14:34 says: "Righteousness (moral integrity) exalts a nation." The same principle holds true for individuals, families, careers, ministries etc.

In 1787 the historian Gibbon listed five reasons for the decline and fall of the Roman Empire. Each is a violation of one or more of the Ten Commandments:

1) The rapid increase of divorce; the undermining of the home which is the basis of society.

2) Ever increasing taxes and the spending of public monies for free bread and entertainments for the people.

3) The mad craze for pleasure, sports becoming every year more riotous and more brutal.

4) The building of gigantic armaments when the real enemy was the decadence of the people.

5) The decay of religion, faith fading into a mere formalism, losing touch with life and impotent to guide the people.[3]

As long as moral truth is considered relative, there is no chance for people (or nations) to see their need of salvation. What would happen if the bricklayer abandoned the use of the square, the level, and the plumb? What if he decided that what is straight to you is not necessarily straight to him? His buildings would lack structural integrity, and would soon collapse as a result. *Do you see why the devil hates the Law and wants to destroy it?*

SMALL GROUP DISCUSSION
QUESTIONS FOR CHAPTER TWO.

1. What is legalism?

2. Can you think of an example of legalism?

3. What is antinomianism?

4. Can you think of an example?

5. What are the effects of antinomianism in the church?

6. Name the three categories of Law in the Old Testament. Explain each one.

7. Who did Jesus say would be called least in the kingdom of heaven? Who would be called the greatest in the kingdom of heaven? Why? (See Matt. 5:18-19)

8. According to Matt. 22:36-40 and Rom. 13:8-10, how are love and law related?

9. What is the relationship between law and grace?

CHAPTER THREE

THE LAW OF GOD
IS WRITTEN
ON EVERY MAN'S HEART

I received a call one day from an organization known as Inner City Impact in Chicago. The man asked me if I would be interested in addressing their youth group at a weekend retreat. I said, "I would love to address your youth group. What would you like me to teach on?" The answer was, "Sexual purity." I gulped, and asked what age group they were and the answer was, "High school." My heart sank as I hung up the phone. I remember thinking to myself, *I would much rather be locked up in a maximum security prison and preach on the love of God, rather than face these young people, and try to convince them that purity is the best way to go.* Please don't misunderstand. I believe with all my heart that this is one of the most critical issues of our day, and it needs to be addressed. My problem was, I had never preached on that particular subject to that particular age group before, and I don't like to preach unless I have something compelling to say.

At the retreat I had approximately 50 girls on my left, and 50 boys on my right. I asked the girls, "How would you like to know the three secrets that will make you the most eligible girl in your entire neighborhood for marriage?" I was met with a resounding, "Yes!" I said, "A real man, a good man, will be looking for three things in a wife: First, someone he can respect, second, someone who is special, and third, someone who is a challenge. Now watch and listen very carefully."

I walked over to the boys and said, "Gentleman, if you had the opportunity to marry one of two women, both are equally beautiful, both are equally talented, both are equally gifted, and both of them have dynamic personalities. In fact, they're identical twins. The only difference between the two is, one of them has had multiple sexual partners, and the other one is a virgin. How many will take the virgin? Raise your hands." Without hesitation, *all of them* raised their hands. I said, "Gentleman, keep your hands right where they are!" I walked back over to the girls and said, "Ladies, I don't care what they're telling you in the back seat of the car on Saturday night, take a good look at 'em now, because there's the naked truth!" I could see many of them turning their heads like curious puppies, obviously thinking to themselves, "Wow, there's a revolutionary concept. I never thought of that before."

I went on to say, "For those of you who are still virgins, just remember that you can always become like the girls who are not, but they can never become like you. As for those who have lost their virginity, I have some good news for you. It's never too late to start living right. The next best thing is 'secondary virginity.' You can decide today to remain celibate. If you have to wait one, two, five, or ten years for the right man to come along, and you tell him you have been waiting for him all that time, I guarantee you he will think you are someone he can respect, you are special, and you are a challenge." They *all* applauded![1]

ABSOLUTE TRUTH

Contrary to those who claim there is no such thing as absolute truth (which apparently is the only thing that is absolutely true), we live in a moral universe with an absolute standard of right and wrong. Every man from the beginning of time until the end of the world, whether or not he has ever read a Bible or ever even heard of Jesus Christ, knows in his *heart* it's wrong to murder, it's wrong to steal, it's wrong to lie, and it's wrong to have another man's wife. He knows it "instinctively." Whether he will admit it or not, that's another story. Which brings me to...

THE ATHEIST AND HIS CONSCIENCE

"A study was done a while back into all the famous atheists of history; Sartre, Kamoo, Nietzsche, Freud, Marx, Madalyn Murray O'Hair . . . and every single one of them had something in common. They either lost their father when they were young, their father abandoned their family, or they had a terrible relationship with their father. That is very interesting because often these doubts aren't reallydriven by intellectual questions, they are being driven by an emotional issue that really blocks them from *wanting* to relate to a heavenly Father because they feel so abandoned, or cheated, or hurt by their earthly father."[2]

Listen to the so-called "intellectual," and finally, an "honest atheist," Aldus Huxley, who speaks for all atheists (whether they like it or not) in this priceless quote:

"I had motives for not wanting the world to have meaning; consequently assumed it had none, and was able without any difficulty to find satisfying reasons for this assumption . . . . The philosopher who finds no meaning in the world is not concerned exclusively with a problem of pure metaphysics; he is also concerned to prove there is no valid reason why he personally should not do as he wants to do. For myself, as no doubt for most of my contemporaries, the philosophy of meaninglessness was essentially an instrument of liberation. The liberation we desired was simultaneously liberation from a certain political and economic system, and liberation from a certain system of morality. We objected to the morality because it interfered with our sexual freedom."[3]

There you have it. Most of the time the "intellectual concerns" people raise when they encounter the claims of Christ are only smokescreens to cover the real issues which are moral. Men love darkness rather than the light, and do not want to relinquish authority of their lives to God.

Humanly speaking when all is said and done, if a person rejects Christianity, ultimately, it is the will *not the intellect* that stands in the way. Jesus said, "If any man is willing to do His (God's) will, he shall know of the teaching, whether it is of God, or whether I speak from Myself" (Jn. 7:17). Matt. 23:37 carries the same idea:

> O Jerusalem, Jerusalem, who kills the prophets and
> stones those who are sent to her! How often I wanted to
> gather your children together, the way a hen gathers
> her chicks under her wings, but you were unwilling.

Paradoxically, no man can come to Christ unless the Father draws him (Jn. 6:44)., and apart from Him, we can do nothing (Jn. 15:5).

According to Rom. 1:18-20, *no one* will stand before God with *any excuse* for ignoring or denying Him:

> For the wrath of God is revealed from heaven against
> all ungodliness and unrighteousness of men, who sup-
> press the truth in unrighteousness, because that which

is known about God is evident within them; for God made it evident to them. For since the creation of the world His invisible attributes, His eternal power and divine nature, have been clearly seen, being understood through what has been made, so that they are without excuse.

In other words, all an honest person has to do is to take a good look at the sun, the moon, the stars, and your own body (which the Bible says, "is fearfully and wonderfully made") to *know* that anything so complex, so perfectly designed and well balanced as is our world and our universe, could in no way have made itself. Only "a fool says in his heart, 'There is no God'" (Ps. 14:1). This, however, is only the general revelation that God exists. There is a huge difference between believing *in* God, and *believing* (and knowing) God!

Intellectual assent is not Biblical faith. There are many people who "believe" the Bible is true, yet continue to live as pagans.

> Not everyone who says to Me, "Lord, Lord," will enter the kingdom of heaven; but he who does the will of My Father who is in heaven. Many will say to Me on that day, "Lord, Lord, did we not prophesy in Your name, and in Your name cast out demons, and in Your name perform many miracles?" And then I will declare to them, "I never knew you; depart from Me, you who practice lawlessness."
> Matthew 7:21-23

The moral Law takes us beyond the general revelation that God exists, and points out the need of a personal relationship with our Creator (Ex. 20:1-3, Gal.3:24). The relationship is based on the fact that I am a sinner, and He is the Savior!

APOLOGETICS

I personally enjoy the art and the science of defending the Christian faith, known as apologetics. The latest discoveries from science, for example, are wonderful for the edification and the building up of the saints. Certainly these intellectual arguments can and do play a part in helping people who have *legitimate* questions and concerns about Christianity. Furthermore, I do believe it would be wonderful if we were all well versed in Hebrew and Greek grammar, Bible interpretation, Bible prophecy, church history, comparative religion, archeology, philosophy, creation science, logic, and debate. However, only one thing is needful. Once you have answered the skeptics questions to the best of your ability (or even if you haven't), there comes a time when you must present the gospel—the greatest apologetic of all!

SPIRITUAL TRUTH TRANSCENDS THE HUMAN INTELLECT

The truth of God's Word is *not* something the human intellect can analyze and synthesize apart from the divine intervention of the Holy Spirit. Only He can open a man's heart *and mind* to "see" the glory of the Gospel. Christianity is not a religion, it's a revelation. First Corinthians chapter two is crystal clear:

> This is what we speak, not in words taught to us by human wisdom but in words taught by the Spirit, expressing spiritual truths in spiritual words. But the natural man receiveth not the things of the Spirit of God: for they are foolishness unto him: neither can he know them, because they are spiritually discerned.1 Cor. 2:13

According to John 16:8, the Holy Spirit's ministry is to "convict the world of sin, righteousness, and judgment." The word *convict* in the Greek speaks volumes:

> To show or prove one of wrong, to detect of hidden things, to correct or chastise in a *moral* sense.

Here is how Noah Webster defined the word "moral" in his 1828 American Dictionary Of The English Language: "Moral 1. Relating to the practice, manners or conduct of men as social beings in relation to each other, and with reference to right and wrong. The word moral is applicable to actions that are good or evil, virtuous or vicious, and has reference to the law of God as the standard by which their character is to be determined."

So, if I want to communicate spiritual truth to a worldly wise man who is incapable of understanding spiritual things, how do I reach him? Romans 2:15:

21

> For when Gentiles who do not have the Law do instinc-
> tively the things of the Law . . . they show the work of
> the Law written in their hearts, their conscience bear-
> ing witness, and their thoughts alternately accusing or
> else defending them.

There is the contact point between the physical and the spiritual, between mortal man and our Eternal Creator. The moral Law (which is spiritual, according to Rom. 7:14), is written on every man's heart!

All the scientific, philosophical, and legal arguments combined, offered by the most able apologists, do not have the power to convict a man of sin.

When it comes to evangelism, the simplest child armed with scripture is more effective than the mightiest Ph.D. without it. In Jer. 23:29 and Heb. 4:12, the LORD speaks through the prophets and the apostles:

> "Is not My word like fire?" declares the LORD, "and like
> a hammer which shatters a rock?"

> For the word of God is living and active and sharper
> than any two-edged sword, and piercing as far as the
> division of soul and spirit, of both joints and marrow,
> and able to judge the thoughts and intentions of the
> heart.

Nothing else even begins to compare to the convicting power of the Ten Commandments, because the sinner knows in his *heart* that what you are saying is not only true, but it is true of himself. What you are doing is exposing a man's deepest, darkest secrets, to the light of God's word. Defining sin and salvation is the church's most powerful apologetic weapon, because it allows the Holy Spirit maximum leverage to do what only He can, convict a person of sin, and consequently, the need of a Savior!

So, rather than trying to prove Noah's flood, or showing the inconsistencies of other religions, the wonders of creation, or any one of a million other things, watch what happens when you get to the seventh commandment with most men. Explain how this commandment condemns even looking at a women with lust, or viewing pornography. WOW! Have you ever had a dentist hit a nerve with a drill?

There is not an intellectual argument in the world, or any other so-called method of evangelism that has the power to shake a man to the core of his soul like God's Law does. I have seen many men break out in a cold sweat, others begin to shake, and still others literally break down in tears of repentance after seeing themselves in the mirror of God's Law! Try explaining (gently and lovingly) that God's moral Law condemns anger as murder, and stealing and lying, even once, as a capitol offense. Sharing the Ten Commandments is the most politically incorrect, in your face, most personal, *and* most loving thing you can say to another human being.

> Better are the wounds of a friend, than the kisses of an enemy (Prv. 27:6).

> Have I become your enemy because I tell you the truth? (Gal. 4:16).

As the late Dr. Walter Martin used to say, "If they don't want Jesus, be sure and leave 'em with Moses!"

In other words, if they don't want salvation as a free gift of grace, be sure and tell them exactly how good they will have to be to save them-selves! This way, you will be able to say (along with the Apostle Paul), "I am innocent of the blood of all men" (Acts 20:26).

SMALL GROUP DISCUSSION
QUESTIONS FOR CHAPTER THREE.

1. Why is there no excuse for unbelief according to Rom. 1:18-20?

2. Paraphrase this verse in your own words.

3. How does knowing this help you when it comes to sharing your faith?

4. Now look at Rom. 2:15. What law is Paul referring to? (See Rom. 3:20, Rom. 3:31, and Rom. 7:7).

5. How does this differ from Rom. 1:20?

6. What do we learn from John 7:17?

7. What is the relationship between the Law and Jesus Christ according to Gal. 3:24?

8. Read Luke 16:19-31. What do you think Jesus means by this?

9. What did you learn from this chapter?

CHAPTER FOUR

WHAT IS WRONG WITH THE MODERN APPROACH TO EVANGELISM?

"In many interviews between reporters and known evangelical leaders, the reporters have asked,

> If evangelicals really are as numerous as the polls indicate, why is it that there seems to be so little impact on the country? Crime continues to increase, divorce statistics climb . . . Is it that there are really not as many evangelicals as you claim, or is it the case that being 'born again' actually makes no difference in how a person lives?

What is the problem? The problem is that the evangelical movement in America is shallow. It speaks of salvation but it does not grapple with sin. And since it does not grapple with sin there can be no true repentance. I am often asked whether we are witnessing a revival today, and I always answer that we are not . . . . There is no revival. There will be no revival until there is an acute awareness of sin, and a genuine turning from it. Until that happens, any national profession of faith will be hollow, and the country will continue to decline, just as Israel did."[1]

To the twenty-first century, post–Judeo-Christian mind (and for the majority of church members), sin is an abstract concept – it's not connected to anything. The problem with many would-be soul winners is that they offer the solution (God's grace) before the impenitent sinner sees there is even a problem. To simply quote Rom. 3:23 and 6:23 to an unregenerate person, and expect them to be convicted by the word *sin*, is like telling someone they are under arrest without telling them what they are charged with! The average man on the street walks away from the typical "Gospel" presentation thinking to himself, "This guy is crazy. I'm not a sinner; I've never murdered anyone!" In the back of his mind he compares himself to the people he hears about on the news, and justifies himself. Willfully ignorant of God's standard of righteousness (sinless perfection), and deceived by the sin nature, he "suppresses the truth in unrighteousness" (Rom. 1:18), and lives in denial. Since no one has defined sin for him (and being content not to search out the matter himself), he lives like he is never going to die. Sin (the key doctrine necessary to understanding the need for salvation), if mentioned at all, is just glossed over.

Most people think that since God is good, He will overlook a few "minor transgressions." That would be like a criminal standing before a judge and saying, "Sure, I've committed a crime or two, but I didn't kill anyone, and you're a good person, can't you just overlook this one thing?" The judge would say, "You're right; I am a good person, and because I am good I *must* punish criminals." Only a corrupt judge would allow a guilty person to escape the due penalty of the law. It is precisely because God *is* good (i.e., perfectly holy) that He must punish sin. To do otherwise would be to deny Himself. That is what the gospel is all about, how God can legally forgive a person who confesses their sin (1 Jn. 1:9).

J.C. Ryle was a preacher's preacher in 19th century England. In his excellent book entitled *Holiness*, Ryle hit the nail on the head with his opening statement, "The plain truth is that a right knowledge of sin lies at the root of all saving Christianity. Without it, such doctrines as justification, conversion, sanctification, are 'words and names' which convey no meaning to the mind. The first thing, therefore, that God does when He makes anyone a new creature in Christ, is to send light into his heart and show him that he is a guilty sinner. The material creation in Genesis began with 'light,' and so also does the spiritual creation. God shines into our hearts by the work of the Holy Spirit, and then spiritual life begins . . . . I believe that one of the chief wants of the church . . . has been, and is, clearer, fuller teaching about sin."[2] The fact is, you cannot understand *any* of the Biblical terms related to the doctrine of salvation in the New Testament apart from the doctrine of sin.

Redemption: A term meaning to release on payment of ransom. The idea is illustrated in buying a slave and setting him free. The question is, free from what? Eph. 1:7: "In whom we have *redemption* through his blood, the forgiveness of *sins*, according to the riches of his grace."

Salvation: A term meaning to be saved, or to be delivered. The question is, saved or delivered from what? Matt. 1:21: "And she shall bring forth a son, and you shall call His name JESUS: for He shall *save* His people from their *sins*."

Justification: A legal term meaning "to be declared righteous." How and why do we need to be declared righteous? Rom. 5:8–9: "But God demonstrates His own love toward us, in that while we were yet *sinners*, Christ died for us. Much more then, having now been *justified* by His blood, we shall be saved from the wrath of God through Him."

Righteousness: An attribute of God Himself, it refers to virtue, integrity, and purity. "For he hath made Him to be *sin* for us, who knew no *sin*; that we might be made the *righteousness* of God in Him" (2 Cor. 5:21).

Sanctification: A term meaning to be set apart. Set apart from what? Acts 26:18: "To open their eyes and turn them from darkness to light, and from the power of Satan to God, so that they may receive forgiveness of *sins* and a place among those who are *sanctified* by faith in Me."

Gospel: Means Good News. Mark 1:15: "The time is fulfilled, and the kingdom of God is at hand; repent (*from sin*) and believe in the *gospel*."

The Cross: Was this not where the body of Christ was broken and His blood shed to satisfy the righteous demand of God's holy Law against *sin*? There is a direct correlation between God's love and the cross. (see Jn. 3:16, Rom. 5:5,6, 8; Gal. 2:20, Eph 2:4,5; 5:2, 25; 1 Jn. 3:16; 4:10; and Rev. 1:5)

There are two primary words used in the Bible to communicate the essence of sin. The first is *hamartia* (ham-ar-tee'-ah), translated in English as "sin." It literally means to "miss the mark and so not share in the prize." This word is well illustrated by a marksman shooting an arrow and missing the bull's eye. Romans 3:23 assures us that all of us have "missed the mark." The second word is *anomia* (an-om-ee'-ah), translated "transgression," which, unlike "missing the mark" (because we were all born imperfect), refers to an act of willful disobedience. That is to willfully, knowingly violate God's Law. So, from these two words we learn that we are *all* sinners by nature, and we are *all* sinners by choice.

27

KEITH GREEN SAID IT WELL . . .

"Unless people are truly convicted of sin, if they don't fully see that they are totally condemned by the requirement of God's Law, then it is virtually impossible to show them the need of a Savior. Why, what would they need to be saved from? fun? That is why our modern Gospel must dwell on 'all the good things God'll do for you if you'd just accept Him!' We can't convince a sinner that he needs a savior by just getting him to admit that, 'Well, generally, yes, I am a sinner.' He must see how the Law of God totally condemns him as a sinner, and then the beauty of the gospel, the glory of the cross, the marvelous power of Christ's blood will be able to penetrate his anxious, waiting mind and heart.

"But because there is so little real conviction of sin brought about by the preaching of our modern gospel, we cannot truly require repentance anymore. If we did, no one would "come forward" at all. For repentance is easy to him who sees how ugly and horrible sin is, but repentance is impossible where the Law does not convince the sinner of his wicked heart, compelling him to turn from his sin into the arms of a waiting, compassionate God. The natural tendency of the flesh is to avoid unpleasantness or discomfort, so we offer people a less confrontational, more indirect approach—something Jesus *never* did."[3]

Walking a person gently and lovingly through the Ten Commandments, and explaining the spiritual application of each one, showing how all of us have broken God's Law in thought, word, and deed, is absolutely, positively, the most convicting (politically incorrect) thing you can say to another human being! And, since hell awaits those who refuse to believe, it is also the most loving thing you can do for someone. "Faithful are the wounds of a friend, but the kisses of an enemy are deceitful" (Prv. 27:6). Sadly, most people are unwilling to discuss these extremely personal issues. So, in order to avoid pain or embarrassment, we offer people a "Gospel" that has little or no conviction of sin. Just *believe* Jesus died for you, pray this prayer, and you're in! I have seen this over and over again by well-meaning, but misinformed people in the ministry.

PARADOXICALLY, ALL WE CAN DO TO GET INTO HEAVEN IS TO BELIEVE IN JESUS

> For God so loved the world, that He gave His only begotten Son, that whoever believes in Him should not perish, but have eternal life. John 3:16

The question is, what does it mean to *believe*, and *what* am I supposed to believe? Even the demons "believe" in Jesus, and they fear Him, but you won't see them in heaven! (Jas. 2:19)

The word *believe* is found in the Gospel of John ninety-six times, more than any other book of the Bible. The word translated "believe" in the English Bible comes from the Greek word *pisteuo*, and is used as a verb; it's an action word! It means: to believe in, to trust in, and to rely upon Christ alone for your salvation. It is derived from the same root word as the word faith. To believe in Jesus, means to have faith in Jesus.

> And without faith it is impossible to please Him for all who come to God must believe that He is, and {that} He is a rewarder of those who seek Him. Heb. 11:6

> And after He had come into the house, the blind men came up to Him, and Jesus said to them, "Do you believe that I am able to do this?" They said to Him, "Yes, Lord." Then He touched their eyes, saying, "Be it done to you according to your faith."
> Matt. 9:28-29

"In the Hebrew language, there is no word for faith, apart from the idea of faithfulness. In our being faithful to Him we find the purpose for which we were created. That is not bondage, that is liberating. Our faithfulness to Him is the key that unlocks the treasure of all that He has given to us."[4] So what does it mean to have faith? In 1 Cor. 4:1-2 we find this answer:

So then, men ought to regard us as servants of Christ and as those entrusted with the secret things of God. Now it is required that those who have been given a trust must prove faithful.

His master said to him, "Well done, good and faithful servant; you were faithful with a few things, I will put you in charge of many things, enter into the joy of your master." Matt. 25:21

Genuine faith *in* Jesus results in a life of faithfulness *to* Jesus. Who were the epistles written to? "Paul, an apostle of Christ Jesus by the will of God, to the saints who are at Ephesus, and {who are} faithful in Christ Jesus." (Eph.1:1) The question now becomes, what does it mean to be faithful?

He who believes in the Son has eternal life; but he who does not obey the Son shall not see life, but the wrath of God abides on him. John 3:36

When the Lord Jesus shall be revealed from heaven with His mighty angels in flaming fire, dealing out retribution to those who do not know God and to those who do not obey the gospel of our Lord Jesus. 2 Thes. 1:7–8

Please note, when we talk about obeying God's commandments, we are talking about practical holiness from a heart of loving gratitude, *not justification by works!* We do not obey Jesus to get saved. Loving obedience is the *result* of our salvation, never the cause of it! See Luke 18:13-14, Rom. 1:17, 3:20-24, 10:9, Gal. 3:24, Eph. 2:8-10, and Titus 2:11.

WHAT AM I SUPPOSED TO BELIEVE?

Who was Jesus? Was He a prophet, a priest, a king, a man, God incarnate, or all of the above?

There are seven "I am" sayings of Jesus in the New Testament. Each one is a clear reference to Exodus 3:14 when God revealed His name to Moses: "I AM WHO I AM." So, when Jesus said, "Before Abraham was born I am," the Pharisees knew exactly what He meant, and they wanted to stone Him for claiming to be God (Jn 8:58,59 & 10:30,31).

But, Jesus did not just *say* things like, "I am the light of the world," He *said*, "I am the light of the world," and then gave sight to a man born blind! He did not just *say,* "I am the bread of life," He *said*, "I am the bread of life," and then fed five thousand people! He did not just *say,* "I am the resurrection and the life." He *said,* "I am the resurrection and the life," and then called forth Lazarus from the dead! Each of the "I am" sayings were accompanied by a miracle which in turn revealed attributes that belong to God alone. For example, the one miracle that Jesus performed more than any other was giving sight to the blind. Compare that to what God said in Exodus 4:11:

> And the LORD said to him, "Who has made man's mouth? Or who makes {him} dumb or deaf, or seeing or blind? Is it not I, the LORD?"

These three "I am" sayings show Jesus to be the Creator, the Sustainer, and the Redeemer of mankind. How about when He said, "Peace, be still," and the winds and the sea obeyed Him? How about, "Destroy this temple, and in three days I will raise it?" He was speaking of raising Himself from the dead! How about when He said, "Your sins are forgiven?" Only God can do those things!

There are hundreds of examples of Christ's divinity in the New Testament, that, however, is beyond the scope of this book. The point is, unless you believe that Jesus was, and is, the Great "I Am" of the Old Testament, you will die in your sin (See John 8:24). Here are just a few more examples in the New Testament.

"In the beginning was the Word, and the Word was with God, and the Word was God. He was in the beginning with God." John 1:1-2

"And the Word became flesh, and dwelt among us, and we beheld His glory, glory as of the only begotten from the Father, full of grace and truth." John 1:14

"I and the Father are one." John 10:30

"Jesus said to him, 'Have I been so long with you, and yet you have not come to know Me, Philip? He who has seen Me has seen the Father'" John 14:9

"And not finding any way to bring him in because of the crowd, they went up on the roof and let him down through the tiles with his stretcher, right in the center, in front of Jesus. And seeing their faith,

He said, 'Friend, your sins are forgiven you.' And the scribes and the Pharisees began to reason, saying, 'Who is this who speaks blasphemies? Who can forgive sins, but God alone?'" Luke 5:19-21

"And after eight days again His disciples were inside, and Thomas with them. Jesus came, the doors having been shut, and stood in their midst, and said, 'Peace be with you.' Then He said to Thomas, 'Reach here your finger, and see My hands; and reach here your hand, and put it into My side; and be not unbelieving, but believing.' Thomas answered and said to Him, 'My Lord and my God!'" John 20:26-28

". . . looking for the blessed hope and the appearing of the glory of our great God and Savior, Christ Jesus." Titus 2:13

SMALL GROUP DISCUSSION
QUESTIONS FOR CHAPTER FOUR.

1. Define redemption, salvation, justification, righteousness, sanctification, gospel, and the cross. How does each relate to sin?

2. What is the difference between being a sinner by nature and a sinner by choice?

3. How do most people view themselves on the moral scale?

4. What can you do to help people see themselves as God sees them morally?

5. What does it mean to "believe" in Jesus?

6. What are we supposed to believe about Jesus?

7. What is the difference between intellectual assent and heart knowledge?

8. List some of the evidences Jesus gave to prove He was God.

9. Read Romans 8:16. What does that mean? Compare it to 1 John
    5:13.

10. What did you learn from this chapter?

CHAPTER FIVE

JESUS CHRIST, THE MASTER EVANGELIST

HEAR YE, HEAR YE, ALL RISE. THIS COURT IS NOW IN SESSION.

Opening statement for the Defense: Your Honor, ladies and gentlemen of the jury, I will now present my case by examining eyewitnesses from the New Testament. These testimonies will provide irrefutable proof that Jesus used a method of evangelism that has been, for all practical purposes, entirely forsaken by modern evangelical methods. In addition, we will provide you (the jury) with expert testimonies from a number of the world's foremost leading authorities in the art and science of Biblical interpretation. This will substantiate our claim, that there is one method of presenting the Gospel that is ordained by God, and as such, cannot be improved upon by man. My final witness will be none other than the Lord Jesus Christ Himself!

FOR MY FIRST WITNESS, I CALL THE RICH YOUNG RULER TO THE STAND.

Rich Young Ruler, will you tell the court your story?

"Well, as Jesus started on His way, I ran up to Him and fell on my knees before Him. I said, "Good teacher, what must I do to inherit eternal life?" "Why do you call Me good?" Jesus answered, "No one is good—except God alone. You know the commandments: 'Do not murder, do not commit adultery, do not steal, do not give false testimony, do not defraud, honor your father and mother.'" "Teacher," I declared, "all these I have kept since I was a boy." Jesus looked at me and loved me. "One thing you lack," He said, "Go, sell everything you have and give to the poor, and you will have treasure in heaven. Then come, follow Me." At this my face fell. I went away sad, because I had great wealth (Mark 10:17-22).

Defense: Your Honor, ladies and gentleman of the jury, this was written for our instruction. A man comes to Jesus Christ and asks, "What must I do to be saved?" The first thing Jesus did was to list 5 of the Ten Commandments. Obviously, the moral Law must have something to do with evangelism! Take another look. The man asks, "What must I do to be saved?" Jesus replied, "You know the Law. Thou shalt not murder, thou shalt not commit adultery, thou shalt not steal, thou shalt not lie, honor your father and your mother." Jesus purposely omitted the tenth commandment which is "Thou shalt not covet." The rich young ruler then says, "All these things I have done since I was a youth. What am I still lacking?" Now comes the fatal blow. Jesus said, "Go sell everything you have and give it to the poor." Rather than quoting the tenth commandment, Jesus applied the text directly to his heart by asking him to do something a covetous person could not do. In order to reveal the true condition of his heart, Jesus used the Ten Commandments as His standard!

Defense: WARREN WIERSBE, TO THE STAND PLEASE . . . .

Mr. Wiersbe, you are recognized the world over as an expert Bible commentator. How do you interpret this story?

Warren Wiersbe: "The rich ruler is a good example of the use of the law to reveal sin and show a man his need of a Savior . . . . [1] Why did Jesus bring up the commandments? Jesus did not introduce the Law to show the young man how to be saved, but to show him that *he needed to be saved* . . . . [2] When Jesus quoted from the second table of the Law, He did not quote the last commandment, 'Thou shalt not covet' (Ex. 20:17). Jesus knew the young man's heart . . . . This young man was possessed by the love of money and he would not let go . . . . He wanted salvation on his terms, not God's, so he turned and went away in great sorrow."[3]

Defense: No further questions.

Judge: Would the State like to cross-examine?

State: Ah, not at this time, your Honor.

Defense: Your Honor, in 1910, A.C. Gaebelein produced a commentary that is still considered one of the most authoritative works ever produced on the book of Matthew. Mr. Gaebelein, do you have anything to add to what Mr. Wiersbe has testified to?

A.C. Gaebelein: I certainly do. Thank you. Your Honor, ladies and gentlemen of the jury . . . "The Lord . . . meets him on his own ground. The ground upon which he stands is the law, and with the law the Lord answers his question. How else could He treat him? The first need for him was to know himself a lost and helpless sinner. If the Lord had spoken of His grace, of eternal life as a free gift, he would not have understood Him at all. The law was needed to make known to him his desperate condition and to lay bare his heart."[4]

Defense: Thank you, Mr. Gaebelein. Your Honor, Jesus said to the rich young ruler, "Go, sell everything you have and give it to the poor." How would that have helped him? Would he have been saved if he had gone out and given everything he had to the poor? Never! In spirit and in truth, this "command" to go and sell all he had and give it to the poor was given to reveal to him (and to us) the fact that his goods were his gods. He was in clear violation of the first (no other gods), the second (no idols), and the tenth (not to covet) commandment. The very Law he thought he kept only revealed the true condition of his heart. "For where your treasure is, there your heart will be also" (Matt.6:21).

State: I object, your Honor. Nothing in the Bible is relevant to the Christian today prior to the Book of Acts!

Defense: Ah, your Honor, Paul said in Galatians 3:24 that, "The Law is our schoolmaster to lead us to Christ that we might be justified (saved) by faith." That was *after* the Book of Acts!

Judge: Overruled!!! Proceed.

Defense: For my next witness, I call the woman at the well. Madam, would you please tell the court your experience with Jesus on that fateful day?

Samaritan Woman: Well, as you know, I'm a Samaritan and a woman. I came to draw water from the well one day, and Jesus asked me, "Will you give me a drink?" (His disciples had gone into the town to buy food.) I said to Him, "You are a Jew and I am a Samaritan woman. How can You ask me for a drink?" (For Jews do not associate with Samaritans.) He replied:

> If you knew the gift of God and who it is that asks you for a drink, you would have asked Me and I would have given you living water. John 4:10

"Sir," I said, "You have nothing to draw with and the well is deep. Where can you get this living water? Are you greater than our father Jacob, who gave us the well and drank from it himself, as did also his sons and his flocks and herds?" (vs. 11,12) Jesus answered:

> Everyone who drinks this water will be thirsty again, but whoever drinks the water I give him will never thirst. Indeed, the water I give him will become in him a spring of water welling up to eternal life. (vs. 13,14)

At this point, I got excited. I said to Him, "Sir, give me this water so that I won't get thirsty and have to keep coming here to draw water" (vs. 15). Jesus said to me, "Go, call your husband and come back" (vs. 16). "I have no husband," I replied. He then said . . .

> You are right when you say you have no husband. The fact is, you have had five husbands, and the man you now have is not your husband. (vs. 17,18)

"What You have just said is quite true, Sir," I replied. "I can see that You are a prophet . . . " (vs. 19). Then, leaving my water jar, I went back to the town and said to the people, "Come, see a man who told me everything I ever did. Could this be the Christ?" (vs. 28,29)

Defense: Your Honor, this woman asked Jesus for the living water, so she would never have to thirst again. The problem here is that she was talking about H_2O, and He was talking about the Holy Spirit. Please note, the woman asked Jesus for a drink, and He did *not* give it to her!

The lesson is clear. The average "would-be" soul winner, upon hearing her request for a drink (completely oblivious to the fact that they were talking about two different things), would have immediately pulled out a tract and started offering her all the benefits of the Gospel before she understood why she needed it! Jesus did not give her the "water," because she did not understand that ultimately her real need was not water, but the "washing with the water through the word" (Eph. 5:26). Specifically, her real need was the conviction, confession, repentance, and forgiveness of her sin!

Because the sin problem had not been dealt with yet, Jesus went right to the heart of the problem. When she said, "Give me a drink," He said, "Go call your husband." On the surface, His answer seems irrelevant. What did calling her husband have to do with getting a drink? Everything! Look again . . .

Jesus said, "Go call your husband." She said, "I have no husband." Jesus said (in essence), "You are correct, Madam. You have had five husbands, and the man you are *living with now is not* your husband!" She brilliantly responded with, "Sir, I perceive that Thou art a prophet!"

What was Jesus doing? Make no mistake about it. Just like the rich young ruler, Jesus was asking this woman to do something an adulteress could not do. The Lord was referring her (and us) to the seventh commandment, which is "Thou shalt not commit adultery." Why? Because from Genesis to Revelation, God's Word assures us that those who do not repent from the practice of sexual immorality will not enter the kingdom of heaven!

> Or do you not know that the unrighteous shall not inherit the kingdom of God? Do not be deceived; neither *fornicators*, nor idolaters, nor adulterers, nor effeminate, nor homosexuals, nor thieves, nor {the} covetous, nor drunkards, nor revilers, nor swindlers, shall inherit the kingdom of God.
>
> 1 Corinthians 6: 9–10

Judge: Would the State like to cross-examine?

State: Ah, no, your Honor. This doesn't exactly fit my theology, but I don't know how to refute it.

Judge: Very well. Call your next witness, Counselor.

Defense: I call Nicodemus to the stand. Nicodemus, you were there. Tell us your story.

Nicodemus: Well, I'm a Pharisee, and a member of the Jewish ruling council. I came to Jesus at night and said, "Rabbi, we know you are a teacher who has come from God. For no one could perform the miraculous signs you are doing if God were not with him" (John 3:2). In reply, Jesus declared:

> Truly, truly, I say to you, unless one is born again, he cannot see the kingdom of God. (vs. 3)

Then I asked Him, "How can a man be born when he is old? He cannot enter a second time into his mother's womb and be born, can he?" (vs. 4)

> Jesus said: I tell you the truth, no one can enter the kingdom of God unless he is born of water and the Spirit. Flesh gives birth to flesh, but the Spirit gives birth to spirit. (vss. 5 & 6)

Defense: Thank you, Nicodemus. You may step down. I would now like to call one of the greatest Bible commentators of the 20th century to the stand. I call Arthur W. Pink. Arthur, what can you tell us about this most curious exchange between Jesus and Nicodemus?

A.W. Pink: Well, here is what I wrote in my commentary on John, word for word: "What the sinner needs is to be 'born again,' and in order to do this he must have a Savior. And it is of these very things our Lord speaks to Nicodemus. Of what value is teaching to one who is 'dead in trespasses and sins,' and who is even now, under the condemnation of a holy God! A saved person is a fit subject for teaching, but what the unsaved need is preaching, preaching which will expose their depravity, exhibit their deep need of a Savior, and then and only then reveal the one who is mighty to save."[5]

Defense: Thank you, Mr. Pink. Your Honor, here again we see the same pattern. Jesus asked Nicodemus to do something he could not do. So, where do we see the Law in this instance? The key word here, is the word *Pharisee*. The typical Pharisee thought his salvation was based on the fact that he was a descendent of Abraham. He believed he was on a one-way trip to heaven, based solely on his national and religious heritage (by keeping the *Law* of Moses). His theology was totally backwards. Nicodemus thought he was an in-law, when in fact he was an outlaw. The Bible assures us that God does not have any grandchildren. According to Romans 3:20, the Law that this Pharisee thought would save him was the very Law that would condemn him!

With that one statement, "You must be born again," Jesus was referring Nicodemus to his misunderstanding of the Law. No one was *ever* saved by keeping it, because the perfect Law demanded perfect obedience. "The Law," as Leon Morris has pointed out, "is the categorical imperative of God, by which men are accused and exposed as sinners."[6] Therefore, Nicodemus had to be born all over again.

Human nature has not changed since the beginning of time, and will remain the same until the end. The people to whom Jesus witnessed to were caught up in the same self-righteousness, self-justification, and love of the world as we are today. The names have changed, but the sin nature has not.

So, what do we learn from these examples?

THESE THREE PEOPLE REPRESENT THE VAST MAJORITY OF THE PEOPLE YOU WILL ENCOUNTER IN WITNESSING

1. Nicodemus believed his salvation was in religion.

2. The woman at the well was blinded by her sin, and unaware of her true spiritual condition.

3. The rich young ruler thought he was a good person.

Jesus referred each of them directly or indirectly to the Ten Commandments.

THERE IS ONE EXCEPTION
TO USING THE LAW . . .

If you meet a person under condemnation, who really believes his past is so bad that God Himself cannot or will not forgive him, *this person does not need the Law.* There is only one thing standing between this person and everlasting life, a crystal-clear understanding of God's grace! Remember the woman caught in the act of adultery in Jn. 8:4? Jesus gave her grace.

Bengel: Those who are broken and contrite Jesus consoles with the Gospel, but to the proud and self-righteous He gave the Law.

Your Honor, before offering my closing arguments, I would like to ask Jesus to reveal the truth one more time. Lord, would You please?

Jesus: "Now there was a certain rich man, and he habitually dressed in purple and fine linen, gaily living in splendor every day. And a certain poor man named Lazarus was laid at his gate, covered with sores, and longing to be fed with the {crumbs} which were falling from the rich man's table; besides, even the dogs were coming and licking his sores. Now it came about that the poor man died and he was carried away by the angels to Abraham's bosom; and the rich man also died and was buried. And in Hades he lifted up his eyes, being in torment, and saw Abraham far away, and Lazarus in his bosom. And he cried out and said, 'Father Abraham, have mercy on me, and send Lazarus, that he may dip the tip of his finger in water and cool off my tongue; for I am in agony in this flame.' But Abraham said, 'Child, remember that during your life you received your good things, and likewise Lazarus bad things; but now he is being comforted here, and you are in agony.' And besides all this, between us and you there is a great chasm fixed, in order that those who wish to come over from here to you may not be able, and {that} none may cross over from there to us.' And he said, 'Then I beg you, Father, that you send him to my father's house—for I have five brothers—that he may warn them, lest they also come to this place of torment.' But Abraham said, 'They have Moses and the Prophets; let them hear them.' But he said, 'No, Father Abraham, but if someone goes to them from the dead, they will repent!' But he said to him, 'If they do not listen to Moses and the Prophets, neither will they be persuaded if someone rises from the dead'" (Luke 16:19–31).

(At this point, pandemonium broke out! Reporters ran to the phones to get the story out as quickly as possible. Jesus Himself had just said that using the Law of Moses in the evangelistic encounter was a more compelling argument for Christianity than someone rising from the dead! The lawyer for the American Counsel for Lies and Ungodliness just hung his head in shame. The judge was banging his gavel, calling for order in the court! When order was finally restored, the judge asked me to proceed, and I closed with this . . . .)

Defense: Your Honor, ladies and gentleman of the jury, Luke 16 is crystal-clear. Jesus, in relating this story, is saying in no uncertain terms that you have a better chance of leading people to Christ by introducing them first to Moses than if their own grandmother came back from the dead to warn them of the judgment to come! By God's grace, Matthew Henry, one of the most respected Bible commentators of all time, understood this last verse perfectly. He said, "Foolish men are apt to think any method of conviction better than that which God has chosen and appointed."[7]

The inevitable result of the knowledge of sin is an overwhelming sense of gratitude for God's past, present, and future grace. This in turn produces a passion for loving obedience and a hatred for sin. At this point, we want to obey God, not to get saved, but because salvation has already been provided; not in a law, but in a Person, and that Person is Jesus Christ!

FOR YOUR INFORMATION

You can know that the Ten Commandments are divinely inspired, because between them and every other religion, philosophy, or system of thought, there is no possible term of comparison. Think about it. Galatians 5:14 (which is a distillation of the Ten Commandments), says: "For all the Law is fulfilled in one word, even in this: 'You shall love your neighbor as yourself.'" If we all cared about each other as much as we cared about ourselves, we would live in a perfect world! I rest my case.

Judge: Does the State have anything at all?

State: Yes, I want to get saved!

Judge: This court is forced to the inescapable conclusion, based on Scripture and reason, that the New Testament is crystal-clear on the place of the Ten Commandments. Beginning with Moses and explaining the New Testament application of each one of the Ten Commandments in the evangelistic encounter, is the most compelling and convicting method of preparing the heart for the message of God's love and mercy. Furthermore, since this is the method that Christ Himself used, and since nobody knows more about evangelism than Jesus, I hereby declare, by the authority of the Word of God, that, in the words of one evangelist,

> Evermore, the Law must prepare the way for the Gospel. To overlook this in instructing souls is almost certain to result in false hope, the introduction of a false standard of Christian experience, and to fill the church with false converts.

Therefore, my judgment is for the Defense. Next case.

SMALL GROUP DISCUSSION
QUESTIONS FOR CHAPTER FIVE.

1. This chapter can be used as a drama to teach the principles of evangelism.

2. According to pages 41 and 42, there are four basic categories that people fall into. What are they, and what Biblical character represents each of them?

3. What should you differently when sharing the gospel with a person who is under condemnation? Why?

4. Why is the good news of Jesus dying for our sins so good?

5. What was the rich young ruler's problem?

6. What problem did the woman at the well have?

7. What problem did Nicodemus have?

8. What did you learn from this chapter?

9. How do we know the Ten Commandments were written by God and not by man?

CHAPTER SIX

DON'T TAKE
MY
WORD FOR IT

I will never forget having dinner one night with a group of elders from a church, which included a man who held a prominent position with the largest evangelical association in the world. He was also a professor at a well known seminary, and had written a book on evangelism that sold over a million copies! During our conversation, I was asked how my (this) book was coming along. I replied, "Very well, thank you." The professor inquired about the subject of my book, to which I replied, "Evangelism." He immediately asked what the premise of my book was. I said, "The main ingredient missing from the modern approach to evangelism is the moral Law, that is what prepares the heart for the Gospel." One of the other men then asked the professor what his position on the matter was. Without hesitation he said, *"Well, that is the classical position!"* In other words, that *is* the consensus of the greatest minds in the history of the church, but it is not necessarily what I believe.

Well, he was right. That is the classical position. The greatest preachers in the history of the church understood how to use the Ten Commandments for the purpose of preparing the heart for the gospel. Yet, this Biblical truth has been, for all practical purposes, entirely forsaken by modern evangelical methods. This is the result of the dominance of liberalism in our seminaries which began around the turn of the 20th century.

The following quotes come from men who have an understanding of God's Word that most of us can only dream of. Humanly speaking, of those who have gone on to be with the Lord, their rewards cannot be calculated yet, because their ministries are still bearing fruit.

I begin with Charles Haddon Spurgeon, who is considered one of the most brilliant men in the history of the church since the Apostles. Charles Spurgeon has more books in print today than any other man alive or dead. He has been gone for over one hundred years!

Charles Spurgeon: "Explain the Ten Commandments and obey the divine injunction: 'show my people their transgressions, and the house of Jacob their sins.' Open up the spirituality of the law as our Lord did, and show how it is broken by evil thoughts, intents, and imaginations. By this means many sinners will be pricked in their hearts."[1]

John Calvin: "We are certainly under the same obligation as they were; for there cannot be a doubt that the claim of absolute perfection which God made for His Law is perpetually in force."[2]

John Wesley: When speaking of those who didn't use the Law as a school-master, Wesley said, "All this proceeds from the deepest ignorance of the nature of the properties and use of the Law. And, proves that those who act thus either know not Christ, are strangers to living faith, or are at least but babes in Christ, and as such are unskilled in the word of righteousness."[3]

Martin Luther: "The first duty of the gospel preacher is to declare God's Law and show the nature of sin. Why? Because it will act as a schoolmaster and bring him to everlasting life which is in Jesus Christ."[4]

D.L. Moody: "This is what God gives us the Law for, to show us ourselves and our true colors."[5]

Matthew Henry: "There is no way of coming to that knowledge of sin which is necessary to repentance, but by comparing our hearts and lives by the Law."[6]

John Newton: (who penned the words to "Amazing Grace") "The correct understanding of the harmony between law and grace is to preserve oneself from being entangled by errors on the right hand and on the left."[7]

John Bunyan: "The man who does not know the nature of the Law cannot know the nature of sin. And he who does not know the nature of sin cannot know the nature of the Savior."[8]

Augustine: "Through the Law, God opens man's eyes so that he sees his helplessness and by faith takes refuge to His mercy and is healed. The Law was given in order that we might seek grace, grace was given in order that we might fulfill the Law."[9]

Jonathan Edwards: "What good is it to have godly principles yet not know them? Why should God reveal His mind to us if we don't care enough to know what it is? Yet the only way we can know whether we are sinning is by knowing His moral law: 'By the law is the knowledge of sin'" (Rom. 3:20).[10]

Spurgeon: "I do not believe that any man can preach the gospel who does not preach the Law. The Law is the needle, and you cannot draw the silken thread of the gospel through a man's heart unless you first send the needle of the Law to make way for it. If men do not understand the Law, they will not feel they are sinners. And if they are not consciously sinners, they will never value the sin offering. There is no healing a man 'till the Law has wounded him, no making him alive till the Law has slain him."[11]

Wesley: "Therefore I cannot spare the Law one moment, no more than I can spare Christ, seeing I now want it as much to keep me to Christ, as I ever wanted it to bring me to Him. Otherwise this 'evil heart of unbelief' would immediately 'depart from the living God.' Indeed each is continually sending me to the other—the Law to Christ, and Christ to the Law."[12]

Martin Luther: "The Law and the gospel are given to the end that we may learn to know both how guilty we are, and to what again we should return."[13]

General William Booth: "The chief danger of the twentieth century will be religion without the Holy Ghost, Christianity without Christ, forgiveness without repentance, salvation without regeneration, politics without God . . . and heaven without hell."[14]

A.W. Pink: "The rest of the scriptures are but a commentary on the Ten Commandments, either exciting us to obedience by arguments, alluring us by promises, or restraining us from transgressions by threatenings. Rightly understood, the precepts of the New Testament are but explications, amplifications and applications of the Ten Commandments."[15]

H.A. Ironside: "But that law so terrible to the sinner, is a law of liberty to the regenerated one, because it commands the very behavior in which the one born of God finds his joy and delight."[16]

Leon Morris: "The law of Moses is not a religion of salvation, it is the categorical imperative of God by which men are accused and exposed as sinners."[17]

Walter Kaiser Jr.: "The classic theme of all truly evangelical theology is the relationship of Law and Gospel. In fact, so critical is a proper statement of this relationship . . . that it can become one of the best ways to test both the greatness and the effectiveness of a truly biblical or evangelical theology."[18]

John MacArthur: "Evangelism must take the sinner and measure him against the perfect law of God so he can see his deficiency. A gospel that deals only with human need, only with human feelings, only with human problems, lacks the true balance. That is why churches are full of people whose lives are essentially unchanged after their supposed conversion. Most of these people, I am convinced, are unregenerate and grievously misled.

". . . We need to adjust our presentation of the gospel. We cannot dismiss the fact that God hates sin and punishes sinners with eternal torment. How can we begin a gospel presentation by telling people on their way to hell that God has a wonderful plan for their lives? Scripture says, 'God is angry with the wicked every day'" (Ps. 7:11, KJV).[19]

Michael Horton: "Here indeed is a revelation of man's final sin, which Luther defined as the unwillingness to admit that he is a sinner."[20]

Kay Arthur: "The Old Covenant is the Law which came by Moses, and, believe it or not, it plays a vital role in bringing a man or woman to Christ. If we would use it more, we would probably not have so many *false* professions of salvation."[21]

Alexander Maclaren on Romans 3:19–26: "Every word of God, whether promise, or doctrine, or specific command, has in it some element bearing on conduct . . .

"But Paul sets forth another view of its purpose here; namely, to drive home to men's consciences the conviction of sin. That is not the only purpose, for God reveals duty primarily in order that men may do it, and His law is meant to be obeyed. But, failing obedience, this second purpose comes into action, and His law is a swift witness against sin. The more clearly we know our duty, the more poignant will be our consciousness of failure. The light which shines which shows the path of right, shines to show our deviations from it. And that conviction of sin, which it was the very purpose of all the previous revelation to produce, is a merciful gift; for, as the Apostle implies, it is the prerequisite to the faith which saves."[22]

Donald Grey Barnhouse on Romans 3:20: "Here we meet by far the most difficult Divine utterance for the human heart to yield to that we have met in the entire epistle. Even those without law— 'Gentiles that have not the law' (of Moses—Rom. 2:14) we find throughout history so many committed to their ideas of what is 'right', that they will desperately fight for their convictions . . . ."It is much easier to detach a Chinese from the analects of Confucius and bring him to a knowledge of Christ, than it is to detach some people, born within the sphere of Christendom, from their hope of salvation by the golden rule. They are astonished when you tell them that Christ did not give them the golden rule as a formula for salvation, but as a means of revealing to man that he is fundamentally crooked (sinful, i.e., full of sin) and that therefore he needed a power outside himself . . . ."The law was a standard that was given in order to convince men of their own hopeless incapacity, so that they might come to God in grace. The law of God is like a mirror. Now the purpose is to reveal to you that your face is dirty, but the purpose of a mirror is not to wash your face. When you look in a mirror and find that your face is dirty, you do not then reach to take the mirror off the wall and attempt to rub it on your face as a cleansing agent. The purpose of the mirror is to drive you to the water. Any other use of the mirror is plain folly. It is by the straight edge of the law of God, whether expressed by Moses or reaffirmed by our Lord Himself, that man may know how crooked he really is, and may turn from the folly of selfeffort to the reality of the life of faith in Christ.

"This new life furnishes us with power which we can never have of ourselves, and which will act within us. May God slay us with the law, in order that we might be raised from the dead by His gospel. For this is the true relationship between the two. Before God can ever give us the gospel, He must slay us with the law. The gospel is the power of resurrection; the law is the power of condemnation; and when the two are put together, they then serve their proper purpose."[23]

William Barclay on James 1:25, 2:10: "All the great men have agreed that it is only in obeying the law of God that a man becomes truly free. So long as a man has to obey his own passions and emotions and desires, he is nothing less than a slave. It is when he accepts the will of God that he becomes really free."[24]

Jamieson, Fausset, Brown on Romans 3:20: "How broad and how deep does the Apostle in this section lay the foundations of his great doctrine of justification by free grace—in the disorder of man's whole nature, the consequent universality of human guilt, the condemnation, by reason of the breach of divine law, of the whole world, and the impossibility of justification before God by obedience to that divine law! Only when these humiliating conclusions are accepted and felt, are we in a condition to appreciate and embrace the grace, next to be opened up. It is that which ascertains what sin is, shows how men have deviated from its righteous demands, and sentences them to death because they have broken it."[25]

Martyn Lloyd-Jones: "So that, finally, we can put it like this. The law was never given to save man, but it was given as a 'schoolmaster' to bring him to the Savior. The whole object and purpose of the law is to show that man can never save himself. Once he has understood the law and its spiritual meaning and content he knows that he cannot keep it. He is undone....It shows us our utter helplessness and hopelessness, and thereby it becomes 'our school-master to lead us to Christ,' the only one who by the grace of God can save us, and deliver us, and reconcile, us to God, and make us safe for all eternity."[26]

Alexander Mclaren: "The voice that spoke from Sinai reverberates in all lands . . . . This voice like a trumpet on that day, waxes louder and louder as the years roll. Whose voice was it? The only answer explaining the supreme purity of the commandments, and their immortal freshness, is found in the first sentence of this paragraph, 'God spake all these words.'"[27]

Gleason Archer: "It was only the misunderstanding and misinterpretation of the law — as a system of merit-earning and self-justification — which is rejected in Romans 3 and Galatians 3 (and related passages). As for the Decalogue (Ex. 20:1–17), the whole basis of its sanctions is stated to be God's act of redemption by grace ('I am the Lord thy God, who wrought thee out of . . . bondage')."[28]

R.C. Sproul: "He (Chemnintz) insists that the Christian church make a clear distinction between Law and gospel, but not a separation! If we see the Law of God as separated from the gospel of God, we would see these two ideas as being intrinsically and fundamentally opposed one to another.

"Now, if you confuse the two ideas: Law and gospel, then what happens is you either eliminate the Law by reducing it to a simple expression of the gospel, or you eliminate the gospel by making it a new law. So, you have to distinguish between them. And what Cheminitz understood as the two great distortions of understanding Christian truth that have plagued the church not just from the first century, but from the garden of Eden, have been the distortions of legalism and antinomianism. Legalism, in its simplest definition, is that error, indeed not just an error, but rank and deadly heresy that teaches that people can be saved through their own acts of righteousness, that people may be saved legally through performing the works of the Law.

"Antinomianism is the heresy that says, because we are not saved by the Law, but by the gospel, not by merit, but by grace, not by works, but by faith, that therefore the Christian life has nothing to do with law, nothing to do with obedience. That's antinomianism. And so, what Cheminitz and Luther were concerned about was this, that if you try to have the gospel in isolation from the Law, you are going to end somehow in antinomianism.

"If you try to have the Law without the gospel, you are going to end in legalism. Cheminitz makes the startling observation that the whole struggle of Israel in history, was the struggle over an understanding of the relationship between these two things, and he starts with Cain and Abel as exhibit 'A'; trying to answer the question, 'Why was it that Abel's sacrifice was accepted by God, and Cain's wasn't?' The answer that Cheminitz gives to that question is, 'because Abel made his offering by faith,' which meant, even in the making of the offering of worship and of praise before God, he came in a spirit of humility; understanding that the only way even this offering would be acceptable to God would be on the basis of divine grace and mercy. On the other hand, Cain was trusting in his performance. (The offering Cain brought represented the work of his own hands.)

"It's not by accident that the two greatest leaders of the sixteenth century reformation, both Luther and Calvin, were both deeply trained students in secular law before they embarked on a career in theology. They were students of jurisprudence, and they had a keen eye for the Old Testament Law, and they saw what the Law was trying to show them, their own inadequacy."[29]

Erwin W. Lutzer: "Christ's answer to legalism is that external obedience to the moral law must be coupled with a corresponding inner attitude of love and honesty. Christ's teaching was not intended to abrogate obedience to the moral law, but to add to its intended spirit."[30]

D. A. Carson: "If you begin (presenting the gospel) with a massive view of God; of His holiness, of the sheer ugliness and odiousness of sin, and of the terrors of judgment, then preaching justification brings immense relief! And with the relief, a sense of gratitude from which a great deal of Christian ethics springs. There is a tremendous amount of Christian ethic that springs from the sheer gratitude to the grace of God. "If on the other hand you barely mention Law, or God, or judgment, or terror, or hell, and then you preach justification, justification is very easily confused with a cheap grace decisionism. Then afterwards, you feel you have to whip people into shape with lots of talk about commitment. The fact that God spends two thousand years from Abraham to the cross, almost a millennium and a half from Sinai to the cross, to teach the function of Law, to bring about a sense corporally in the people of God of the nature of transgression, and of the futility of human effort, and the critical importance of recognizing how lost we are.

"So, if then we now start evangelizing without presupposing any of that, or without people knowing any of that, we just dive right into a Jesus who meets your needs, however *you* define your needs, then it's not too surprising we start having distorted views on justification, and a lot of other things as well. If all we learn from chapter three of Galatians is the vastness of the fact that the Law prepares the way for the gospel, but do not grasp how and why it prepares the way, we will not apply it to people's lives appropriately. And, then we will end up with a cheap gospel, and then we will end up with such a diluted justification that there will be tremendous pressures to redefine justification, which is precisely what is going on now."[31]

Erwin W. Lutzer: " I always start at Sinai before I take them to the cross!"[32]

SMALL GROUP DISCUSSION
QUESTIONS FOR CHAPTER SIX.

1. Do you have a favorite quote, and why?

2. Read Matt 22:36-40 and Gal. 5:14. The Bible itself says that its main message can be distilled into a single truth. What is that truth? Now read A.W. Pink's quote at the bottom of page 49. What are the implications of Pink's statement?

3. How does the moral Law apply to evangelism according to John MacArthur on page 50?

4. What is man's final sin according to Michael Horton (and Martin Luther) on page 50?

5. Many people mistakenly believe that you have to obey the Ten Commandments to get into heaven. How does Gleason Archer help us to explain that on page 53, and Leon Morris on page 50?

6. There are people who do not believe that the concept of Law has anything to do with New Testament Christianity. What would you say to that person?

7. What are the proper uses and applications of the Law in our day and age?

8. What did you learn from this chapter?

CHAPTER SEVEN

PRESENTING THE GOSPEL
IN
THE POWER OF THE SPIRIT

THE WINDOW SALESMAN

Ideally, I like to build a rapport with someone before I drop this bomb in his or her life, but that is not always possible. One day I was expecting a window salesman to come by and give me an estimate on two new windows for my home. The phone rang, and it was Bob from the window company. He said he was just around the corner and wanted to come by a little early. I was in the study, and my children were eagerly looking out the living room window in anticipation of his arrival. Shortly thereafter, I heard the children cry out, "He's here, he's here."

We all watched as the man got out of his car. Like any good salesman, he began to "read" our house. He was looking for clues that might reveal something about us. Obviously, if a salesman can find a common denominator between himself and his client, he may be able to improve his chance of making the sale. Nothing wrong with that, just good salesmanship. Well, our house is easy to read. There is a big cross in the living room window that lights up, and the bumper sticker on the car in the driveway said, "STUDY FOR YOUR FINAL EXAM; READ THE BIBLE!" As I said, our house is easy to read. Now, I'm not making this up. This is exactly how it went, word for word.

I walked out to the side of the house and opened the gate. As my eyes met his, his first words were, "My dad was a Christian." I asked, "Are you here from the window company?" He said, "And, my sister was a missionary!" I said, "You *are* from the window company!" He said, "Oh, yes. I'm from ____ Window Company, and I'm here to measure your windows."

He then proceeded to tell me all about his dad and his sister. I enjoy a good sales presentation, so I hear him out. After about five minutes I asked, "Bob, can we look at the windows now?" When he came back with his estimate, he went right back to his dad and sister.

After a couple minutes I asked, "Ah, excuse me, Bob, but, can I ask you a personal question?" He said, "Sure." I said, "You've been telling me a lot about your dad and your sister, but where do *you* stand with God?" He said, "Oh, I'm fine."

At this point, I got excited, because I knew I had a golden opportunity standing right in front of me in my own yard. I said, "So, you believe in God?" "Oh, yes," he replied. I followed with, "If you died tonight, would you go to heaven or hell?" "I'd go to heaven," he said. "On what basis?" I asked. "Oh, I've been a good person," was his reply. I asked, "Do you see your need of God's forgiveness?" He said, "No, I've never murdered anyone." I said, "I suppose if God compared you to Adolph Hitler, you'd probably compare very favorably. But, is that the standard God is going to use? Is He going to compare you to the worst person who ever lived and say, 'Compared to him you look pretty good. Come on in?'" Bob shrugged and said, "I don't think so." "Well, what standard is God going to use?" I asked. Bob's reply was, "I don't know; I don't think anyone knows." Now, I *really* got excited!

I said, "Bob, I'm a chaplain at the Cook County Jail, and there are ten thousand men locked up there, and they're all charged with a crime. If they're found guilty, they'll be judged according to the law. If you're driving down the road going twenty-five miles an hour over the limit, and you run into the man who wears the star, *you* too will be judged by the law!

Psalm 19:7 says, 'The Law of the LORD is perfect, converting the soul.' Do you want to know how you can know that the Ten Commandments were written by God and not by man? If man wrote 'em, there'd be ten commandments and a thousand amendments!

THE FIRST COMMANDMENT IS: YOU SHALL HAVE NO OTHER GODS BEFORE ME

Stated positively, that means you *shall* 'Love the LORD your God with all your heart, mind, soul, and strength.' That means from the day you were born until the day you die, you would never have put anything before God.

So, what does it mean to love God? Jesus said, 'If you love Me you will obey My commands.' But, God is perfect. Followed to its logical conclusion, to obey that commandment, according to God's standard, would require perfect obedience, which is another way of saying sinless perfection. No *mere* man has ever loved God like that!

If the greatest commandment is to 'love God with all your heart,' then the greatest sin cannot be murder. The greatest sin must be to not love the God who created you more than the things He created!

THE SECOND COMMANDMENT IS:
THOU SHALT NOT MAKE UNTO THEE ANY GRAVEN IMAGES

"You are not to make a god with your hands or with your mind. I have people tell me that my god is a god of love; he would never send anyone to hell. I agree with them. Their god would never send anyone to hell, because their god doesn't exist. He's a god made in their own image. The Bible says that, 'God is a consuming fire,' who has a passion for justice, holiness, righteousness and truth, who will by no means clear the guilty, but will hold every man accountable for every idle word that he speaks."[1]

THE THIRD COMMANDMENT IS:
YOU SHALL NOT TAKE THE NAME OF THE LORD IN VAIN

When a man stubs his toe, he usually takes the name God or the name Jesus; the name that is above every other name, the name which represents a blessing, and uses it as a curse.

Ancient Jews were so fearful of breaking this Law he dared not even speak the name of God, because the commandment goes on to say, 'the LORD will not leave him unpunished who takes His name in vain.'

THE FOURTH COMMANDMENT IS:
REMEMBER THE SABBATH TO KEEP IT HOLY

The idea here is to take one day out of seven, and to set aside all your worldly amusements, and any effort to better your position in this world, and rest. And, in that rest, acknowledge the God who created you, the God who sustains you, and the God who purchased your salvation with 'His own blood' (Acts 20:28).

THE FIFTH COMMANDMENT IS:
HONOR YOUR FATHER AND MOTHER

Why is honoring your father and your mother such a big deal? When you dishonor your father or mother, you dishonor God, because He is the One who told us to honor our parents. The condition of our nation today is nothing more than a reflection of the condition of our families; as goes the family, so goes the nation. When you dishonor your parents, you effectively break the chain of command through which God's blessings flow. Abraham Lincoln said: "The strength of a nation lies in the homes of its people."

THE SIXTH COMMANDMENT IS:
THOU SHALT NOT MURDER

Jesus said, "You have heard that it was said, 'You shall not murder...' but I say to you that whoever is angry with his brother (or calls him empty headed or a fool) will be in danger of judgment and the fires of hell'" (Matt. 5:21, 22). When someone does something wrong to you, and you 'decide' not to forgive that person, you have already crossed the line of sin. Jesus taught that we are to forgive even as we have been forgiven (Matt. 6:14,15). Secondly, when you choose not to forgive someone, you are putting yourself in the judgment seat of Christ; you are judging that person unworthy of forgiveness, which only God has the right to do. God says, 'Vengeance is mine; I will repay' (Rom. 12:19). Thirdly, refusing to forgive someone makes you a hypocrite, because you desire God to forgive you for a lifetime of sin, and yet you won't forgive someone else's (see Matt. 18:23-25). Sadly, sometimes the very things you refuse to forgive in others (sin), you may be guilty of yourself.

THE SEVENTH COMMANDMENTS IS:
THOU SHALT NOT COMMIT ADULTERY

Jesus said, "You have heard that it was said, 'You shall not commit adultery.' But I say to you that whoever looks at a woman to lust after her has committed adultery already, in his heart" (Matt. 5:28). Because 'Only man looks on the outer appearance; God looks on the heart' (1 Sam. 16:7).

THE EIGHTH COMMANDMENT IS:
THOU SHALT NOT STEAL

People are not thieves because they steal; they steal because they are thieves. Do you know how much you have to steal to be a thief? *Anything*! It's not the value of the thing, it's the principle of the thing. Jesus said, 'Whatever you do to the least of these my brethren you do to Me' (Matt. 25:40). The Bible says that thieves will not inherit the kingdom of God (1 Cor. 6:9,10).

THE NINTH COMMANDMENT IS :
THOU SHALT NOT LIE

How many lies do you have to tell to be a liar? The same number of times Adam and Eve had to eat the forbidden fruit to be found in rebellion against God and worthy of death – just once. God means what He says, and, He says what He means. Revelation 21:8 says, 'All liars, their part will be in the lake of fire and brimstone which is the second death.' If you're born once, you'll die twice. If you're born twice, you'll only die once.

THE TENTH COMMANDMENT IS:
THOU SHALT NOT COVET

Stated positively, it means: 'Be content with what you have' (Heb. 13:5b). That is, be content with what you can make with your own hands and your own mind. You are not supposed to desire what already belongs to your neighbor; including his house, his car, his wife, his title, his position, or his bank account."

At this point I asked again, "Bob, do you see your need of God's forgiveness?" He hung his head and said, "Yes!" I went on to say . . .

THE GOSPEL

"In the Old Testament, an animal was offered as a sacrifice for sin. The animal had to be perfect, that is, without spot or blemish; symbolic of moral purity. The spot was inherited, and the blemish was acquired. When the virgin Mary was impregnated, not by the seed of man, but by the Holy Spirit, what was begotten nine months later was God in a human body. Because Jesus was not born of the seed of Adam, He had no inherited sin (spot). And, because He kept the Law I just described, He had no acquired sin (blemish). That is why the Bible refers to Him as 'The Lamb of God without spot or blemish' (1 Pet. 1:19).

When Jesus died on the cross, because He had no sin of His own, His death satisfied the righteous penalty of the Law. God can legally declare sinners not only not guilty, but righteous, by virtue of the fact that an innocent substitute was provided on our behalf.

HOW DOES CHRIST'S DEATH
APPLY TO YOU?

While living in the Chicago area, I became engaged to the young lady who is now my wife, Susan. While it was the Lord's idea in the first place, I still wanted the blessing of my future in-laws who lived in Nevada. My fiancé flew out a few weeks before I did. When I arrived, they were expecting me. I knocked on the door, and without hesitation they invited me in. Later that night we had a wonderful dinner together. A few hours later I was escorted to my own private bedroom, and was told to, 'Make myself at home.' The next day my future in-laws said, 'You're going to need to get around, so here are the keys to the car.'

Can you imagine what might have happened if I had knocked on the wrong door, a perfect stranger, and asked for food, a place to stay for the night, the keys to their car, and their daughter's hand in marriage? The sandwich may have been achievable, but the rest would have been out of the question! However, I was accepted and treated like their own son, because I knocked on the right door, I came in the right name, and I had the right motive—love! That is precisely, how it works with God.

Therefore having been justified by faith, we have peace with God through our Lord Jesus Christ, through whom also we have obtained our *introduction* by faith into this grace in which we stand; and we exult in hope of the glory of God. Rom. 5:1-2

In the same way, when you come to God the Father in the name of His Son, Jesus, you are 'accepted in the beloved' (Ephesians 1:6). We are called 'children of God' now (Phil. 2:15, 1 Jn. 3:1, 2, 10; 5:2), and are one of the family! We become 'co-heirs with Christ' (Rom. 8:16-17)!"

I do not know what happened to Bob, but I can tell you this – many grown men have broken down in tears of repentance after hearing God's Law presented in love. And, many others have said, "I have been in church all my life, and never really understood the Gospel until today. Thanks!"

SMALL GROUP DISCUSSION
QUESTIONS FOR CHAPTER SEVEN.

1. Recite the Ten Commandments in order.

2. What are some key questions to ask before you share the gospel?

3. When asked, "If you died tonight, would you go to heaven or hell?" Most people say, "I'm going to heaven!" When asked, "On what basis?" They will say, "Because I'm a good person; I've never murdered anyone!" How do you help this person?

4. How does the death of Christ apply to you?

5. Give a simple illustration of grace.

6. What does the Bible mean by, "To whom much is given, much is required?"

7. What do you think God is trying to tell you in this chapter?

8. This week share the gospel with at least two people. Share your experiences with one another. Pray for those you've shared with before and after your encounter. Remember only God can open a person's heart and mind to the gospel. Your mission is to simply be obedient.

CHAPTER EIGHT

THE PERFECT LAW
OF
LIBERTY

If you recall, it was *after* God set the Israelites free from Egyptian slavery (a picture of slavery to sin), that He gave them the moral Law. William Barclay, the great Scottish theologian, in his commentary on the book of James said this,

> He (James) calls it the Law of liberty; that is, the Law in the keeping of which a man finds his true liberty. All the great men have agreed that it is only in obeying the law of God that a man becomes truly free. So long as a man has to obey his own passions and emotions and desires, he is nothing less than a slave. It is when he accepts the will of God that he becomes really free.[1]

When the LORD says "No" to one thing, He is saying "Yes" to something better. When God says "Thou shalt not lie," He is by implication saying "Thou shall tell the truth." The Ten Commandments, like a coin, have two sides. On one side we see the Law of condemnation and death (2 Cor. 3:7), and on the other we see the perfect Law of liberty (James 1:25 and 2:10). You are either under the condemnation of the Law, or you are free to obey by the power of the Holy Spirit.

God expects His people to walk in holy obedience, not to get saved, but because salvation has already been provided; not in a law, but in a person, and that person is none other than the Lord Jesus Christ.

Consider the wealth of liberating knowledge found in this preamble to the Law:

> Then God spoke all these words, saying, "I am the LORD your God, who brought you out of the land of Egypt, out of the house of slavery. You shall have no other gods before Me." Exodus 20:1-3

First of all, consider the implications of the "I" in Exodus 20:2. This seemingly insignificant little *personal pronoun*, sets you free from the bondage of . . .

1. Atheism: The idea that there is no God. So, how does an atheist account for the universe in which we live? Nobody + nothing = everything! What an empty life that must be!

2. Agnosticism: The idea that man is incapable of knowing if God exists. To know God is to have real purpose in your life!

3. Polytheism: The Hindu doctrine of many gods. At last count they had 330 million gods. I don't know about you, but I have trouble with names as it is!

4. Pantheism: The "New Age" (which is really not new at all) belief that God is all, and all is God.

5. God being an obscure power or an impersonal force (i.e., the "Higher Power" of Alcoholics Anonymous).

THE NEXT STOP IN OUR TOUR
OF THE HOLY LAND IS THE WORD *LORD*

In Hebrew, this word (LORD) is a name. It consists of four consonants, YHWH (pronounced *yood hay vav hay*), and no vowels. It represents the most holy and proper name of God. Theologians call it the Tetragrammaton.

To the ancient Jew, this name was so feared and revered they dared not even speak it for fear of breaking the third commandment. This commandment states that "he who takes My name in vain will not go unpunished" (Ex. 20:7). As a result, the true pronunciation has been totally lost, but the meaning has not. It comes from the same root as the "I Am" of Exodus 3. Here, God appeared to Moses in the burning bush and gave him his commission to deliver the Israelites. Moses, fearing even his own people would not believe him, asked God, "Who should I say sent me; what is Your name?" At this point God said to Moses . . . ,

> "I AM WHO I AM"; and He said, "Thus you shall say to the sons of Israel, 'I AM has sent Me to you.'"
>
> Exodus 3:14

"I AM" is a repetition of the verb "to be." It means the Eternal, Self-Existent One; the God who is, the God who was, and the God who always will be, from eternity past, to eternity future, without beginning and without end!

THE FIRST LAW OF LIBERTY

When God said, "Thou shalt have no other gods before Me," He was saying, "You *shall* love the LORD your God with all your heart, soul, mind and strength" (Mk. 12:30). Jesus said essentially the same thing when He said, "Seek first the kingdom of God and His righteousness and all these things shall be added unto you" (Matt. 6:33).

HERE IS WHY GOD IS WORTHY

In the beginning God created the heavens and the earth. And the earth was formless and void, and darkness was over the surface of the deep; and the Spirit of God was moving over the surface of the waters. Then God said, "Let there be light"; and there was light." (Gen. 1:1-2)

Then the Lord God formed man of dust from the ground, and breathed into his nostrils the breath of life; and man became a living being. And the Lord God planted a garden toward the east, in Eden; and there He placed the man whom He had formed (Gen. 2:7-8).

Then the Lord God said, "It is not good for man to be alone...SO the Lord God caused a deep sleep to fall upon the man, and he slept; then He took one of his ribs, and closed up the flesh at that place. And the Lord God fashioned into a woman the rib He had taken from the man, and brought her to the man (Gen. 3:18,21).

From the section you just read, the words "LORD GOD" are used many times. The LORD GOD formed, the LORD GOD planted, the LORD GOD said, the LORD GOD caused, the LORD GOD fashioned, the LORD GOD took, the LORD GOD made, the LORD GOD commanded the man saying, "From any tree of the garden you may eat freely; but from the tree of the knowledge of good and evil you shall not eat, for in the day that you eat from it you shall surely die" (Gen. 2:16,17).

The LORD GOD, YHWH is our God. He is the one who has created all things. He put everything in its place. He has given all things purpose, from the stars in the heaven to the birds in the air. From the waters that move on the earth, to the blood that flows in your veins.

It is YHWH your God who has given you life and sustains you, who gives you food, who sends the wind, the rain, and the sun. The earth, even all the universe and all that is in it, was made by Him for His pleasure.

Therefore, He alone is worthy of honor, of praise, of devotion, and of adoration. No one and nothing else is worthy of being worshiped, adored, or trusted as God.

Because He is holy, awesome, mighty, pure, and sovereign, He is worthy of worship. Because He is the creator, the sustainer, the redeemer, He is worthy of worship. Simply, because of who He is; He is worthy of worship. This is why Exodus 20:3, "You shall have no other gods before Me." For there are no other Gods and therefore He alone is the only Sovereign, the only Lord, the only God.[2]

So, what does this have to do with liberty? Everything. The first commandment answers the most profound questions any man can ask, namely, *Who am I? Where did I come from? Why am I here? and, Where am I going?* The identity crisis is settled once and for all in the first commandment. When you know who you are in relation to who God is, you find the purpose for which you were created. That is not bondage, that is liberating.

According to 2 Cor. 5:20, Christians are "ambassadors for Christ." An ambassador is the highest ranking official representing one nation (kingdom) to another. As representatives of God on earth, we are to be fully devoted followers of our Lord Jesus Christ. Our mission is to be faithful in bringing the good news of salvation to a lost and dying world. This gives us an awesome responsibility, a great privilege, and the ultimate purpose for living! God has entrusted us with the secrets and the mysteries of the universe, and "To whom much is given, much will be required" (Lk. 12:48). How does that set you free? For a man to be satisfied (free from insignificance), he needs three things: Someone to love, something to do, and something to hope for. How's this for a purpose statement . . .

But you are a chosen race, a royal priesthood, a holy nation, a people for God's own possession, that you may proclaim the excellencies of Him who has called you out of darkness into His marvelous light. 1 Peter 2:9

THE SECOND LAW OF LIBERTY

When God said, "Thou shalt not make unto thee any graven images," He was saying, "God is spirit, and those who worship Him must worship in spirit and truth." John 4:24

The first commandment tells us Who we are to worship, and the second tells us how: "In spirit and in truth." That is, by faith and according to His Word, the Bible. The second Law is a warning against false religion.

Over six billion people now inhabit the earth, and the vast majority of them "believe in God." Most of these "believers" identify themselves with one of the five major world religions: Christianity, Islam, Hinduism, Buddhism, and Judaism.

Many people, unfamiliar with comparative religion, mistakenly believe that they are all basically the same, all worship the same God, and as a result, believe there are "many ways to heaven." Nothing could be further from the truth. The fact is, they are all mutually exclusive. They all claim to be divinely inspired, and all have vastly different definitions of who God is, and equally differing views of "salvation." That being the case, there are only two logical conclusions: Either all of them are wrong, or one is right and the others are wrong. "If you step out into the middle of a busy street, it's either you, or the bus; it can't be both!"[3] 1 Tim. 2:5 says, "There is one God, and one mediator also between God and men, the man Christ Jesus." The one thing that separates Christianity from the rest, is salvation by grace!

CAN A PROPHET LIE?

I will never forget one evangelist who told this story. He was entering a Muslim country and was asked to present his passport to the

69

customs' agent. The question was posed, "For what purpose do you want to enter my country; what is your business?" He answered, "I am an evangelist." The agent said, "I would like to ask you one question. What do you think of Mohammed?" The whole room became dead silent as all the other customs' officials turned to hear his answer. The evangelist said, "Sir, I would like to ask *you* a question." The agent replied, "All right." "Can a prophet lie?" the evangelist asked. The agent thought for a moment, and answered, "No, a prophet cannot lie." "Mohammed was a prophet?" the evangelist asked. Answer, "Yes." Then the evangelist asked, "Mohammed said Jesus was a prophet?" Answer, "Yes." "Jesus said He was God. If Jesus was right, Mohammed was wrong. And, if Jesus was wrong, Mohammed was still wrong, because Mohammed said Jesus was right!" The agent stamped the evangelist's passport and said, "Get out of here!"

Why it is that the name *Jesus* can clear out a room faster than any other name? You can mention the names of any other so-called religious leaders, and no one gets upset. Why is it that in many places of the world you can be imprisoned, tortured, dismembered, or murdered for teaching about Jesus? All Jesus did was say things like, "Love your enemies; if your enemy is hungry, feed him; if he is thirsty, give him a drink; if he takes your shirt, give him your coat, too" (Matt. 5:40, 44; Rom. 12:20). No one has ever spoken with that kind of love before or since. So, why is it that just the mention of the name *Jesus* causes so much hatred? The answer is found in John 3:20:

> For everyone who does evil hates the light, and does-not come to the light, lest his deeds should be exposed.

If Christianity is true, then worshiping the correct God correctly is the most liberating truth you will ever find. As you can see, all gods are not the same.

SHOP, COMPARE, AND SAVE

Buddha said, "I am a teacher in search of truth," and Jesus said, "I am the truth" (John 14:6).

Confucius said, "I never claimed to be holy." Jesus said, "Which one of you convicts Me of sin?" (John 8:46).

Mohammed said, "Unless God covers me with a cloak of mercy I have no hope." Jesus said, "I am the resurrection and the life. He who believes in Me, though he die, yet shall he live" (John 11:25).

Neither Buddha, Confucius, Mohammed, nor Moses ever claimed to be God. They all said God is this way, go this way; and Jesus said . . .

I am the way, the truth and the life, no man comes to the Father but by Me. John 14:6

THE THIRD LAW OF LIBERTY

When God said, "Thou shalt not take the name of the Lord in vain," He was also saying, "Those who honor Me, I will honor." 1 Sam. 2:30b

As Christ's ambassadors, everything we do reflects on our Head of State. We are God's representatives on earth, and as such, we are to strive for holiness in everything we think, say, and do.

Jesus taught us to pray, "Our Father who art in heaven, holy be Thy name, Thy kingdom come, Thy will be done on earth as it is in heaven." To hallow the name of God is to love, honor, and obey Him. "Everyone therefore who shall confess Me before men, I will also confess him before My Father who is in heaven. But whoever shall deny Me before men, I will also deny him before My Father who is in heaven." Matt. 10:32-33

THE FOURTH LAW OF LIBERTY

Remember the Sabbath to keep it holy.

Hebrews 4:9 says, "There remains therefore a Sabbath rest for the people of God." When Jesus died on the cross He said, "It is finished." The word finished means, "Paid in full." God purchased our salvation with His own blood (Acts 20:28)!

While we live in this world (the valley of the shadow of death) we have great reason to be troubled, but thanks to Jesus Christ we have even greater reason not to be! Our future is as bright as are the promises of God!

> Let not your heart be troubled; you believe in G o d , believe also in Me. In My Father's house are many mansions; if it were not so, I would have told you. I go to prepare a place for you. And if I go and prepare a place for you, I will come again and receive you to Myself; that where I am, there you may be also. John 14:1–3

1 John 5:13 says, "These things I have written to you who believe in the name of the Son of God, in order that you may know that you have eternal life." Now that is how I spell r-e-s-t. Death has no sting, and the grave has no victory (1 Cor. 15:55). I can *rest* assured that my salvation is based not on my performance, but on what Christ has done for me. My eternal home is bought and paid for by the blood of Christ. My final destination is secured by Jesus.

Real freedom is freedom from the guilt and the power of sin. Living in the light of eternity is one of the most liberating truths you will ever find! Here is a perfect example:

> By faith Moses, when he had grown up, refused to be called the son of Pharaoh's daughter; choosing rather to endure ill-treatment with the people of God, than to enjoy the passing pleasures of sin; considering the reproach of Christ greater riches than the treasures of Egypt; for he was looking to the reward. Heb. 11:24–26

THE FIFTH LAW OF LIBERTY

> When God said, "Honor thy father and thy mother," He was saying submit to authority that all may go well with you.

Why is honoring your father and your mother so important? God Himself is a picture of the family: Father, Son, and Holy Spirit. The foundational structure of every society is based on the family unit.

The reason our nation is in trouble is not because of crime, drugs, violence, divorce, etc. Those are only symptoms of the real problem. Our nation is in trouble because our churches are in trouble, and our churches are in trouble because our families are in trouble, and our families are in trouble because the men who head up those families have failed to take the role of spiritual leaders in their homes. They have failed to teach their children to honor and submit to authority by example.

THE SIXTH LAW OF LIBERTY

When God said, "Thou shalt not murder," He was saying, "Forgive and you will be forgiven" (Matt. 6:14).

Do you know what is the number one psychological condition is of those who are admitted into mental institutions? Anger, which is rooted in unforgiveness. When you refuse to forgive someone, you are the one in bondage. When you choose to forgive someone, you are the one who gets *set free*. One of the greatest Christians who ever lived was the Apostle Paul. Here is his secret to peace and happiness:

> And so, as those who have been chosen of God, holy and beloved, put on a heart of compassion, kindness, humility, gentleness and patience; bearing with one another, and forgiving each other, whoever has a complaint against anyone; just as the Lord forgave you, so also should you. And beyond all these things {put on} love, which is the perfect bond of unity. And let the peace of Christ rule in your hearts, to which indeed you were called in one body; and be thankful. Colossians 3:12–15

What is the cost of breaking this command? In the 20th century alone, between World War I, World War II, Korea, Vietnam, Hitler, Stalin, Mao, abortion, drunk drivers, murder, suicide, and sexually transmitted diseases, etc., it has been estimated that 500 million people were murdered, which is more than in all the previous 6,000 years of recorded history combined! The 21st century began with a bang when 4,000 civilians were murdered on September 11, 2001. *Statistically,* we will not survive another century!

THE SEVENTH LAW OF LIBERTY

When God said, "Thou shalt not commit adultery," He was saying, "A man shall leave his father and his mother and cleave unto his wife!"

The cost of breaking this command? In the last thirty years, so-called civilized people have murdered more than 50 million unborn children worldwide. In Africa alone, it is estimated that in the next ten years, 30 million people will die of the A.I.D.S. virus! And, the number one incidence of poverty in America is single women with children. No man can calculate the cost or the pain related to sexual immorality. Remember Sodom?

History tells us that in 165 B.C., a Greek king by the name of Antiochus Epiphanies sacrificed a pig on the holy altar before the temple in Jerusalem. This was referred to as an "abomination of desolation." That is something that is so unholy, so sacrilegious, that it utterly desolates (spiritually) an object or place.

The Bible says that "your body is the temple of the Holy Spirit" (1 Cor. 6:19). To take your body (the temple of God), and to join it in an unholy act, is analogous to the abomination of desolation. That is why David pled for God not to take the Holy Spirit from him in Psalm 51 after he had committed adultery with Bathsheba. Sexual immorality of any kind is one sin that will bring judgment and bondage faster than any other. How does that enslave me? The lust of the flesh (like fire) is never satisfied (Prv. 27:20). If you are not satisfied, you don't have peace; if you don't have peace; you're not free. Adultery is one of the highest acts of treason a man can commit against God and his family. When Potiphar's wife was trying to seduce Joseph in the 39th chapter of Genesis, (long before the Ten Commandments were written) Joseph said:

> There is no one greater in this house than I, and he (Potiphar) has withheld nothing from me except you, because you are his wife. How then could I do this great evil, and sin against God? Gen. 39:9

The solution to the epidemic of immorality in our world, and its horrific consequences is simple. Here is the perfect Law of liberty: "Nevertheless, because of sexual immorality, let each man have his own wife, and let each woman have her own husband." 1 Cor. 7:2

THE EIGHTH LAW OF LIBERTY

When God said, "Thou shalt not steal," He was saying,
"It is more blessed to give than to receive." Acts 20:35b

Any idea what the number one crime is in America? Retail theft. The cost? Billions. Who pays for it? We all do. The liberating principle behind this law is found in Ephesians 4:28:

Let a man work with his own hands that he might not have to steal any longer and that he might have to give to those who are in need.

Let us remember that God commanded man to work *before* the fall. Work is a good thing. God says, "If any man won't work, neither should he eat" (2 Thess. 3:10). And, "if a man will not provide for his own family..., he is worse than an unbeliever" (1 Tim. 5:8). Welfare was not a tax burden to the ancient Hebrews.

When Howard Hughes died, his estate was valued at over $1 billion. A reporter doing a story on Hughes contacted one of the accountants who handled the estate, and asked, "How much did he leave?" The answer was, "All of it." Do you know how much of that money Howard took with him when he died? None of it!

On the other end of spectrum, there was a man from nineteenth-century England by the name of George Mueller. George dedicated his life to caring for orphans. At the peak of his ministry, he was caring for ten thousand children! Imagine if you can the job and the expense of providing housing, education, health care, clothing, and food for ten thousand children a day! By today's standards he raised millions of dollars, not for himself, but for the children. It is reported that Mueller died with less than $100 in the bank. Out of all the money he raised, do you know how much he took with him? All of it, he sent it all ahead (see Matthew chapter 25).

In the spiritual realm, whatever you keep you lose, but whatever you give away you keep. As the late Jim Elliot once said, "He is no fool who gives what he cannot keep, for that which he can never lose."

THE NINTH LAW OF LIBERTY

When God said, "Thou shalt not lie," He's saying, "You shall know the truth and the truth shall make you free." Jn. 8:32

By letting my "yes be yes" and my "no be no" (Jas. 5:12), I am reflecting His faithfulness. When I tell the truth, the Lord delights in me, which in turn fills me with joy. My conscience is clear, my sleep is sweet, and I am free from the guilt and the power of falsehood and lies. Whenever I am tempted to sin, one of the most profound *truths* that comes to my rescue is the heart knowledge that sin always *lies*. It always promises pleasure, but it only produces pain! We will do well to remember that Satan is called "The father of lies," and Jesus said, "I Am the Way, the Truth and the Life." Jn. 14:6

Since lying is so commonplace in our world, it is inconceivable what would happen if everyone always told the truth. What would happen if everyone stopped lying tomorrow? God only knows. Much of our judicial system and our political system is based on lies. In many cases, it is the best liar who wins. But not for long . . .

Getting treasures by a lying tongue is the fleeting fantasy of those who seek death. Prv. 21:6

There are many people who would never think of committing murder, adultery, or stealing, but think nothing of lying. After all, lying isn't such a big deal, is it? May I remind you that the first sin on earth occurred when the serpent *lied* to Eve? That was the day when the covetousness of Adam and Eve embraced the lie of Satan, and the whole earth was cursed as a result of one *little* lie!

THE TENTH LAW OF LIBERTY

When God says, "Thou shalt not covet," He was also saying, "If we have food and clothes, with these we should be content." 1 Tim. 6:8

I remember seeing John Rockefeller on the news when I was just a child. He was being asked by reporters, "You're already a billionaire, Mr. Rockefeller; how much more do you need?" The answer was, "Just a little more, son, just a little more." Lest you think covetousness is no big deal, it was Lucifer's lack of contentment that turned him into Satan. The principle of liberty found in this verse is learning to be content. John Piper said it well, "God is most glorified when we are most satisfied in Him."

IN CONCLUSION

"But that law so terrible to the sinner, is a law of liberty to the regenerated one, because it commands the very behavior in which the one born of God finds his joy and delight."[3]

"So I will keep Thy law continually, forever and ever. And I will walk at liberty, for I seek Thy precepts. I will also speak of Thy testimonies before kings, and shall not be ashamed. And I shall delight in Thy commandments, which I love." Ps. 119:44-47

SMALL GROUP DISCUSSION
QUESTIONS FOR CHAPTER EIGHT.

1. How is it possible for the Ten Commandments to be the Law of condemnation and death in one sense, and the perfect law of liberty in another? (See H.A. Ironside on page 50, and Barclay on page 52 for help.)

2. What does the first commandment have to do with our true identity and purpose in life?

3. Explain the difference between the first and the second commandments.

4. What does it mean to worship God in spirit and in truth?

5. When it comes to salvation, what is the one thing that separates Christianity from all other religions?

6. Share a time when you received or extended grace to someone in your own life.

7. Read Heb. 11:24-26. How does living in the light of eternity help us now?

8. What should motivate us to share the gospel?

9. What is the difference between the spirit and the letter of the Law? (See Matt. 5:21, 22 & 5:27, 28.)

10. How does sin enslave you? How is obedience liberating?

CHAPTER NINE

IF GOD IS REALLY THERE, WHY IS THERE SO MUCH EVIL IN THE WORLD?

The number one objection people raise against God is based on the question of evil. If God is God, why doesn't He remove all the evil people? It is a good thing He does not. If He removed all the evil people using His standard, none of us would be left!

Nevertheless, the question of evil is a legitimate question that deserves an answer, and the Bible provides it. The answer is only understood when we see it in the light of the spiritual struggle that has been raging for untold thousands of years between the forces of darkness and the Prince of Peace. It began not in the Garden of Eden, but in Heaven. In Ezek. 28:12-17b, God reveals the mystery of iniquity, and allows us to see exactly what happened before time began:

> Thus says the Lord, "You had the seal of perfection, full of wisdom and perfect in beauty. You were in Eden, the garden of God; every precious stone adorned you . . . . Your settings and mountings were made of gold; on the day you were created they were prepared.
>
> You were anointed as a guardian cherub, for so I ordained you. You were on the holy mount of God; you walked among the fiery stones.
>
> You were blameless in your ways from the day you were created, until unrighteousness was found in you.
>
> By the abundance of your trade you were internally filled with violence, and you sinned; therefore I have cast you as profane from the mountain of God.
>
> And I have destroyed you, O covering cherub, from the midst of the stones of fire. Your heart was lifted up because of your beauty; you corrupted your wisdom by reason of your splendor.

When God created the angels, He created one who was "full of wisdom and perfect in beauty." He was known as the "anointed cherub." I don't know about you, but I have never seen an angel. I do know, however, that they are *not* Caucasian females with long blonde hair, nor are they little babies with wings. According to the Bible, angels are extremely powerful creatures, capable of performing feats of strength far beyond any mortal. In 2 Kings chapter 19, we read the account of an angel that slew 185,000 men from the Assyrian army in one night!

If an angel suddenly appeared in your church next Sunday, no one would have their heads in the air. Their faces would be in the dust! In the Garden of Gethsemane, Jesus said He could have called 12 legions of angels (Matt. 26:53), which would have been enough sword power to destroy the entire Roman army in one day. The real battle, however, is "not against flesh and blood, but against the rulers, against the powers, against the world forces of this darkness, against the spiritual {forces} of wickedness in the heavenly places."

To get more on the story of what happened with Lucifer, we turn to the prophet Isaiah, written 750 years before Christ came to earth. In Isa. 14:12-14 we read:

> How you have fallen from heaven, O star of the morning, son of the dawn! You have been cut down to the earth, you who have weakened the nations! But you said in your heart, "I will ascend to heaven; I will raise my throne above the stars of God, and I will sit on the mount of assembly in the recesses of the north. I will ascend above the heights of the clouds; I will make myself like the Most High."

There you have it. The first sin in the universe—covetousness. Lucifer became discontented as the "guardian cherub, full of wisdom and perfect in beauty," he wanted to be worshiped! It was then that his name was changed from Lucifer (which means the light one) to Satan (which means the adversary).

THE REBELLION IN HEAVEN

It is believed (based on Rev. 12:4), that Lucifer convinced 1/3 of the angels to follow him instead of God. So, here we have 1/3 of the angels in opposition against God. The question is, what should He do about it? Look at His options. He could have vaporized them instantaneously. He could have crushed the rebellion with a word! The problem with that approach would be obvious. If the Creator had simply wiped out the fallen angels, the worship in heaven would have been tainted by fear. We are told in 1 John 4:18-19 that . . .

> There is no fear in love; but perfect love casts out fear, because fear involves punishment, and the one who fears is not perfected in love. We love Him, because He first loved us.

Even though God is sovereign, one thing He cannot do, is make someone love Him. Forced love is a contradiction in terms. If God were to violate your free will here, true love would no longer be possible. So, God implemented the plan ordained before the foundation of the world. That is where you and I come in. We are exhibit "A" to all the host of heaven, that God is love.

THE GARDEN OF EDEN

A close look at what happened in the Garden of Eden is most revealing. God created a small planet and set up a test for all creation to see. Man was placed in a perfect environment. Adam and Eve were created with a conscience, a free will, and without sin. In Genesis 2, the Lord God gave them everything they needed to live in abundance. He provided Adam with a beautiful helpmate and told them to "Be fruitful and multiply." He said, "From any tree of the garden you may eat freely." As God was about to leave them alone for their honeymoon (my paraphrased version), He turned around and said, "Oh, by the way, there is just one thing, just don't eat from the tree of the knowledge of good and evil, for in the day that you eat from it you shall surely die. Have a great day!"

When the Lord forbid them to eat from the tree of the knowledge of good and evil, they were now put in the position where they could be morally tested. The presentation of a choice to obey or disobey was now present. All the angels in Heaven are watching God's plan of redemption unfold in real time. So, what happened? In Gen. 3:

They both took from its fruit and ate; then the eyes of both of them were opened, and they knew that they were naked.

Adam and Eve chose to disobey their Creator, and you and I would have done exactly the same thing. God warned them in advance that sin would result in death. Question: Didn't God know that all this would happen beforehand? The answer is of course! That is why Rev. 13:8 says, "the Lamb (Jesus), slain from before the foundation of the world." In this light, John 3:16 has never been more glorious:

For God so loved the world, that He gave His only begotten Son, that whoever believes in Him should not perish, but have eternal life.

SO, WHAT DOES ALL THIS HAVE TO DO WITH THE LAST EIGHT CHAPTERS?
BRING IN THE ARK OF THE COVENANT

"And the seventh angel sounded; and there arose loud voices in heaven, saying, 'The kingdom of the world has become the kingdom of our Lord, and of His Christ; and He will reign forever and ever.' And the twenty-four elders, who sit on their thrones before God, fell on their faces and worshiped God, saying, 'We give Thee thanks, O Lord God, the Almighty, who art and who wast, because Thou hast taken Thy great power and hast begun to reign.'

"And the nations were enraged, and Thy wrath came, and the time came for the dead to be judged, and the time to give their reward to Thy bond-servants the prophets and to the saints and to those who fear Thy name, the small and the great, and to destroy those who destroy the earth.

"And the temple of God which is in heaven was opened; and the ark of His covenant appeared in His temple, and there were flashes of lightning and sounds and peals of thunder and an earthquake and a great hailstorm" (Rev. 11:15-19).

As we see from Revelation 11, there is a temple in heaven. At some point God's people will be escorted to this temple and be allowed to look into the Holy of Holies. On earth, this was a place that no ordinary man could ever see. Only the high priest could enter there, and then, only once a year to make atonement for the sins of the people. The walls, the floor, and the ceiling were covered with gold. And, inside was the ark of the covenant.

God's greatest attributes (besides the fact that He is omnipotent, omniscient, and omnipresent), are His holiness and His love. In heaven, the ark of the covenant will serve as a perpetual reminder that God purchased the church with His own blood (Acts 20). The ark of the covenant contains the Ten Commandments. They are covered by the mercy seat, which is sprinkled with the blood of Jesus Christ. The whole story of man's fall into sin, and God's forgiveness through the blood sacrifice of His Son is memorialized by the ark, which portrays James 2:13: "Mercy triumphs over judgment."

In order for God to prove His point (rather than destroying Lucifer and the fallen angels when they rebelled in heaven), God is going to let sin run its course— almost. The New Testament teaches that the war of Armageddon will be the war that ends all wars. And, just before this planet is completely destroyed by fire, God is going to stop it. Jesus said, "Unless those days were cut short, no flesh would be saved" (Matt. 24:22). This will allow mankind and the angels to see, once and for all, the inevitable outcome of sin. So, when it is all said and done, there will never be another rebellion in heaven. No one will ever question God's integrity, His right or ability to rule the universe, His motives, His justice or His love again.

The staggering truth is that even the angels who have spent their entire existence in the presence of God are amazed at what a mortal man will do to please the God he has never seen!

> In the same way, I tell you, there is joy in the presence of the angels of God over one sinner who repents. Luke 15:10

Can you imagine how God feels when His people praise Him, and pray to Him in the secret closet of prayer (i.e., when no one is looking)? In Rev. 5:8 we discover that our prayers are precious to God:

> And when He had taken the book, the four living creatures and the twenty-four elders fell down before the Lamb, having each one a harp, and golden bowls full of incense, which are the prayers of the saints.

The church is God's chosen instrument to prove to the angels, the demons, and the world, that His love is perfect. Look at Eph. 3:8-11:

> To me, the very least of all saints, this grace was given, to preach to the Gentiles the unfathomable riches of Christ, and to bring to light what is the administration of the mystery which for ages has been hidden in God, who created all things; in order that the manifold wisdom of God might now be made known through the church to the rulers and the authorities in the heavenly places. This was in accordance with the eternal purpose which He carried out in Christ Jesus our Lord.

The Ark of the Covenant is God's throne! He sits above the mercy seat, which sits above the Ten Commandments. This throne will serve as a perpetual reminder of His perfect justice, and His perfect mercy. No one will ever question His authority, or His love again.

SMALL GROUP DISCUSSIONS
QUESTIONS FOR CHAPTER NINE.

1. Who is responsible for all the evil in this world?

2. What would happen if God removed all the evil people in our world? How many would be left?

3. Why can't God force someone to love Him?

4. What purpose does the ark of the covenant serve in heaven?

5. Why is God going to allow sin to run its course?

6. What does God want us to learn from Job?

7. The Christian has three enemies, the world, the flesh, and the devil. How does each one affect us negatively? Which one gives you the most trouble? Why, when, and how?

8. What is the significance of Rev. 5:8?

9. According to Eph. 3:8-11, what is the function of the church?

10. What is God saying to you in this chapter?

CHAPTER TEN

THE FEAR OF MAN
VS.
THE FEAR OF GOD

Sharing the Gospel, now that you know how, is not a question of fear, but of love. The real question is, "Do I love my neighbor enough to tell him the truth?" Statistically, 95% of people who claim to be Christians have never even attempted to lead another person to Christ, and 71% of them think it is wrong to interfere with another person's belief system. Much of this is based on ignorance on how to present the gospel, and fear, which is rooted in pride (people do not want to be rejected). Proverbs 29:25 says, "The fear of man is a snare, but he who trusts in the Lord will be set on high." A.W. Tozer once said:

> We who preach the Gospel must not think of ourselves as public relations agents sent to establish good will between Christ and the world. We are not diplomats but prophets, and our message is not a compromise but an ultimatum![1]

The fear of man is a trap. The word "trap" in Hebrew was used literally or figuratively, as in this case, for a noose. The word picture is that of a hunter who sets a noose for an animal. 1 Peter 5:8 says:

> Be of sober {spirit,} be on the alert. Your adversary, the devil, prowls about like a roaring lion, seeking someone to devour.

The hunter is Satan and the hunted is the Christian. His goal is to keep the church quiet. He has no need to focus on the world, because they don't have anything to say anyway. It is only the church that has information that he does not want the world to hear. Satan spreads the net, and the fear of man drives people into it. Sometimes it's blatant, sometimes it's very subtle. We smile when we should frown; we laugh when we should remain silent; or worse, we remain silent when we should speak.

The Bible has a lot to say about the fear of man. The father of our faith, Abraham, was willing to give up his wife to another man, not once but twice, because he feared what man might do to him. His son, Isaac, did the same thing with his wife, Rebecca. The first king of Israel, Saul, was one of the most pathetic cases in all the Bible. The Word says that he feared the people more than God, and God rejected him as king. Three times in Matthew chapter 10 it says: "Do not fear them." And, in the 28th verse Jesus said:

> And do not fear those who kill the body, but are unable to kill the soul; but rather fear Him who is able to destroy both soul and body in hell.

In Isaiah 57:11, the Father speaking this time, said:

> Whom have you so dreaded and feared that you have been false to Me, and have neither remembered me, nor pondered this in your hearts? Is it not because I have long been silent that you do not fear Me?

As if God is saying, "Who is this man that you are so afraid of, that you have not been true to Me? Let him step forward. I'd like to get a good look at this dude Myself. He must really be something!"

INSTITUTIONS
OF HIGHER LEARNING?

I hear of college students in secular colleges and universities, who are so intimidated by their atheistic professors that they dare not speak up for their faith for fear of being ridiculed publicly. Some of these "Nutty Professors" have so many degrees, they don't have any temperature left! I read of one incident where a college professor had a brand-new class, and on the first day he asked, "Has anyone in this room ever seen God?"

(Imagine the intimidation that must exist in this type of atmosphere.) He went on with, "Has anyone ever heard God? Has anyone ever touched God? You see, there is no God!" I wish I could talk to one of those nutty professors, because I would like to ask him a few questions. I'd like to ask, "Professor, can I ask the class a question? Has anyone here ever seen the professor's brain? Has anyone ever heard

88

the professor's brain? Has anyone ever touched the professor's brain? Well, then, based on the professor's own logic, we are forced to the inescapable conclusion that our professor is brainless!"

MAY I BE EXCUSED, PLEASE?

In the Old Testament, you were excused from war for anyone of three reasons: (1) If you had just married a wife, (2) If you had planted a vineyard and had not tasted the fruit of the vine, or (3) If you were afraid. Why would being afraid excuse you? I believe it must surely be that if a man was afraid, the morale of one man had the potential of destroying the morale of the entire army.

When God commissioned Gideon to go to battle, He said (in effect), "Gideon, I want you to go to battle, and I'm going to guarantee you the victory. The only thing is, you have too many men. If you win with this many men, you may try to touch the glory, and the glory belongs to Me. I want you to tell everybody who's afraid to go home." He had 32,000 men, and 22,000 of them jumped up and said, "ALRIGHT!" and went home!

IN JOHN 5:44, JESUS SAID:

How can you believe, when you receive glory from one another, and you do not seek the glory that is from the {one and} only God?

Jesus is saying, how can you possibly be a Christian if you live for the praise of men, but you are not seeking to honor the living God?

Sometimes when I am in church on Sunday morning I become so overwhelmed when the worship is being offered up, and I think of where the Lord has taken me from, and the fact that all I really deserve is hell. Sometimes I just close my eyes and lift my hands, which is the universal gesture of surrender, and also the universal gesture of victory. There are people who mistakenly associate this with a particular sect of Christianity. But, I associate it with Paul's letter to Timothy where he said, "I want men everywhere to lift up holy hands unto the Lord" (1 Tim. 2:8). After a service one day, a lady came up to me and said, "I wish I had the courage to raise my hands in church." I did not quite know what to say, because while I knew what the problem was, I did not want to embarrass her. This lady was afraid of being perceived as a religious fanatic in her own church!

The fear of man is idolatry, which is rival worship. Idolatry is placing any created thing before the Creator, and it is an abomination to God. Listen to what the LORD says in Isaiah 51:12:

> I, even I, am He who comforts you. Who are you that you are afraid of man who will die, and of the son of man who is made like grass.

I don't know about you, and I don't mean to brag, but if a piece of grass was stalking me and about to jump me, I wouldn't be afraid at all. In fact, I would not be afraid if there were an entire bail of hay behind me! God is saying in essence, "Let's look at it in perspective. Why are you afraid of a man who is like grass? A man can't save you, and a man can't condemn you." "Strength and courage are necessary equipment for the prophet of God with the message of salvation, which implies judgment for those who reject it."[2]

Generally speaking, in America, church discipline is virtually nonexistent. The reason? Pastors and elders are afraid of offending people. The thinking is, if we offend people they might leave and go to another church. Preaching is weak in many churches for the same reason. I remember inviting one of our neighbors to church one day. I was preaching that Sunday, and, to the best of my knowledge, she had never stepped foot in a church other than the one she grew up in. Her response was a little unusual. She asked, "You won't offend me, will you?" I said, "Well, no. I'll try to offend everybody the same."

Do you realize that Jesus could not be offended? Jesus could not be offended because He had no ego, no pride; He was self-less. We, on the other hand, are easily offended. Why? Because we are filled with pride. To the degree we are easily offended, that is the degree we are walking in the flesh, and not in the Spirit.

I believe one of the main reasons that people reject the Gospel of Jesus Christ is not that they can't believe, it's that they won't. Jesus said, "If any man is willing to do my will, he will know of my teaching, whether I speak of Myself or whether I speak for God" (John 7:17).

Many people know that if they become Christians, that would require a radical change in their lifestyle. And how would they be perceived by their friends, relatives, neighbors, and co-workers? I don't believe in peer pressure, I believe in pressuring my peers.

MIRACLE ON 26th STREET

I was walking down California Avenue in Chicago, while going to minister at the Cook County Jail. I was feeling filled with the Spirit of God and joy! Then, two men walked out right in front of me and began walking in the same direction. It was broad daylight, about high noon. Now, I'm not exaggerating. One of them was about 6'8", 300 pounds, and the other one was about half his size. We were walking along, and as we were walking we passed by a young lady standing at a bus stop. The big guy looked at her and said, "Boy, you are one ____ ____!" I shook my head in disbelief, and without even thinking, I blurted out, "Boy, you must really attract 'em with that approach!" He turned around and said, "Huh?" I said, "They must just be hanging all over you with that approach." He said, "I got a few." His little buddy laughed, and the big guy countered with a look that quieted him instantly. I asked, "Do you have any idea what you just did?" He said, "Huh?" I said, "Do you have any idea what you just did? What you just said to that young lady, you just said to Jesus Christ. Jesus said, 'Whatever you do to the least of these my brethren you do to Me' (Matt. 25:40). Do you have any children?" He said, "Ya." I said, "Well, if I'm walking down the grocery aisle with my 2-year-old in the cart and somebody walks by and says, 'Boy, that's the ugliest kid I've ever seen in my life.' Do you know who that would hurt? It wouldn't hurt my child; she wouldn't even know what that means. I'm the one who would take the hit on that. If on the other hand, while I'm looking at the price of bread, she drops her toy and someone picks it up and gives it to her and says, 'What a beautiful child,' she's just glad to have her toy back. I'm the one who says, 'Thank you very much.' Ya get it? Do you see this (pointing to my chaplain's ID)? Do you know who I am? I'm not the police, I'm not a judge, I'm a chaplain. Can I ask you a personal question?" He said, "Ok." I said, "Are you a gang member?" He looked both ways, then down, shrugged his shoulders and said, "Ya." I said, "I'm a Christian. Jesus Christ is offering me forgiveness for my sin, a purpose in life, and eternity in heaven. If I leave my church to join your gang, what's your gang going to do for me?" He looked at me, looked at the jail, and said, "Probably just end up here, or catch a bullet in the head." I said, "No thanks, man. I'm stickin' with Jesus!" I then shared the Gospel with him. He walked away saying, "Man, I really need to think about this."

The point to this story is not my boldness. I didn't have time to think about this, it just happened. The point is, when this man said what he said to this young lady, what he was really saying was, "I am hurting so badly; I need to be loved so bad; I am so empty inside, that I am willing to insult this lady just so my buddy will think I'm cool!" This is the other side of the fear of man, he wanted the praise of men.

CAN I HELP YOU, SIR?

I walked into a retail store with my wife our five children. A man walked up to us and we began talking. In less than 60 seconds, right in front of my wife and children, he said, "I don't know what the hell to think about that." I cringed inside, but didn't say anything. In less than 30 seconds, he said it again! This time I looked him right in the eye and said, "Excuse me, sir, do you know that hell is a real place?" Poof, he disappeared! When I hear somebody use the name of the Lord in vain, it cuts me like a knife. Friends, we need to have a civil defense plan. We need to know in advance what we are going to do when we hear this kind of thing. I'm not a golfer, but for some reason this illustration comes to mind. If you're out on the golf course and somebody in front of you hits a shot that goes way off in the wrong direction, and he curses the name of God, I couldn't help myself. I'd probably say something like, "Hey, why don't you try praying *before* you make the shot next time!"

Does the Bible say, "Study to show yourselves approved unto man"? No. It says, "Study to show yourselves approved unto God. A workman who does not need to be ashamed, rightly dividing the word of truth" (2 Tim. 2:15). Most Christians can quote the verse that says, "We have not been given a spirit of fear, but of power and of love and of a sound mind" (2 Tim. 1:7). But, precious few can quote the next one. It says, "Therefore," and you all know that whenever the Bible says, "Therefore," you have to find out what it's there for, because it's there for a reason. It says, "Therefore, do not be ashamed of the testimony of our Lord" (vs. 8a).

WHO, ME?

There are people who are so hardened by pride and by the deceitfulness of sin, they are so afraid of being perceived as weak, that they cannot say, "I love you. I was wrong. Please, forgive me," to their own family members! If I am speaking to you, then you need to repent. You need to tell your loved ones, "I'm sorry. I was wrong. I love you. Please, forgive me!"

I think I've defined the problem for you. Now, I would like to talk about the solution. How do we get delivered? First of all, I don't believe anyone is immune from this spiritual weakness known as the fear of man. I think all of us have it, to one degree or another, but I want you to understand something. The only way to get delivered is to have a proper concept of God!

THE GUN THAT KILLS WITHOUT BULLETS

The fear of man is just like a gun without bullets. You can scare a lot of people with a gun, even if it has no bullets. However, it's power is purely psychological. It has no real power. The fear of man is just like that. It's not there. It's all in the mind! If someone puts a gun to my head and says, "Renounce Christ, or I'll take your life," I would have to say, "You mean you're threatening me with heaven? Go ahead, make my day!" For the Christian, death is not the end; it's the glorious beginning! You haven't found anything worth living for, until you've found something worth dying for!

Deliverance from the fear of man, like any other sin, is a work of grace. A work of grace is something only God can do. Paradoxically, our part must be factored in. The text says, "The fear of man is a snare, but he who trusts in the Lord will be lifted up" (Prv. 29:25).

How do you learn to trust the Lord? As Christians, we are not asked to leap into blind faith or to commit intellectual suicide. In fact, the Word of God says, "Faith is the substance of things hoped for and the evidence of things not seen" (Heb. 11:1).

God says He is eternal and He created for all to see. All you have to do is take a good look at the sun, the moon, and the stars, and ask yourself, "Where did it all begin and where does it end?" And, if there is an end, what's there, a brick wall? If there is a brick wall there, what's on the other side? God really is eternal, and He gave us all the proof we would ever need to believe it!

JESUS, THE WONDERFUL COUNSELOR

I had a man come to my office for counseling. After about fifteen minutes I said, "We're done." He said, "We are?! But, you didn't talk to me about my drug problem." I said, "You don't have a drug problem." He said, "I don't?" I said, "No." He said, "But, you didn't talk to me about my alcohol problem." I said, "You don't have an alcohol problem." He said, "I don't?" I said, "Nope." He said, "But, you didn't talk to me about my marriage problem." As you may have guessed by now, I told him he did not have a marriage problem. In utter astonishment, he said, "This is incredible. I've only been here for fifteen minutes, and I don't have any of these problems anymore?" I said, "No." He asked, "Well, what's my problem?" I said, "Your drug, alcohol, and family troubles are only symptoms of the real problem. Your real problem is, you don't know who God is. When you find out who He is, then you will know who you are. When you know who you are, in relation to who He is, then your drug and alcohol problems will disappear. And, when you come home, your wife will find you a lot more lovable!"

WHAT DOES A THREE-THOUSAND-YEAR-OLD UNCIRCUMCISED PHILISTINE HAVE TO DO WITH ME?

Remember the story of David and Goliath? The Philistines on one side represent the world. They send out their champion, the best the world has to offer, and they challenge the people of God to do battle. What's at stake? God's name, God's word, and God's reputation!

Saul, the king of Israel, and the Israelites all "believed" in God. Well, "even the demons believe in God" (James 2:19). David came on the scene, heard the giant's threats, and understood that the battle belonged to the Lord. And, he, after all, was one of God's covenant people. He was in a covenant relationship with the living God! They had a blood relationship, and David understood that whoever cursed him, cursed God! Jesus said the same thing, "Whatever you do to the least of these My brethren you do to Me" (Matt. 25:40). The Israelites believed in God, but David believed God! How do you get delivered from the fear of man? Don't just believe in God, begin to believe God and His word!

I had a man in my office who got wonderfully, gloriously saved. He was bubbling all over the place. At one point in our conversation, I asked, "So, what are you going to do now?" His reply was classic. He looked up, scratched his chin, and said, "I think I'll read the Bible, and I'll do what it says!" I started laughing from the depths of my soul. I said, "Man, if everybody would just read the Bible and do what it says, we would live in a perfect world!"

Do you want the power of God to flow through your life, and get delivered from this worldly mind-set? Read the Bible, and do what it says. God says that if we honor Him, He will honor us (1 Sam. 2:30).

When the presence of God is so strong in your life, willful disobedience will no longer be an alternative. How do you get this presence of God in your life that is so strong, that sin will no longer hold you in its power, and to deny Jesus publicly would be unthinkable? I'm glad you asked, because I have a couple of ideas on that.

IN MATTHEW 10:32,33, JESUS SAID:

"Therefore whoever confesses Me before men, him I will also confess before My Father who is in heaven. But whoever denies Me before men, him I will also deny before My Father who is in heaven."

The first time I read this verse I got scared. I knew that if I was really a Christian, I would have to tell all my friends about Jesus. The problem was, I was afraid of being labeled a "Jesus Freak" or a "Religious Fanatic." The upside was that I knew "we" were right! The only question was, how do I explain it to others? I was still fearful of what my friends would say. This verse, however, is infinitely more powerful than "friends" are.

It seemed to me that God was saying that if you are a Christian, there is no such thing as neutral ground. You're either part of the problem, or part of the solution. You're either an asset, or a liability. "He who is not with Me is against Me; and he who does not gather with Me scatters" (Matt. 12:30).

So, I prayed and said, "Lord, if you'll take that fear of man away from me, I'll never miss an opportunity to speak for You. Wherever I am, whatever I'm doing, if I feel Your elbow in my ribs, I'll speak up." At the time of that prayer I had no idea that 1 John 5:14 said this:

> Now this is the confidence that we have in Him, that if we ask anything according to His will, He hears us. And if we know that He hears us, whatever we ask, we know that we have the petitions that we have asked of Him.

I "believed" in Jesus when I was fifteen years old. I "believed" so strongly, I "believed" I would have died for Him rather than renounce my faith. My problem was, I wasn't living for Him. I realize now that ours is not the "god of the dead; He's the God of the living" (Mk. 12:27). He didn't want me to die for Him (necessarily); He wanted me to live for Him. He did answer my prayer, and consequently, "I am no longer ashamed of the gospel, for I know it is the power of God unto salvation to all who believe" (Rom. 1:16). Some people do think I'm a "Jesus Freak," and some do think I'm a "Religious Fanatic," but God calls me son!

DINNER FOR TWO?

Picture this: You go out to a nice restaurant with your spouse. The hostess comes up and asks, "Table for two?" Your spouse replies, "We would like separate tables, please." You ask, "What are you talking about?" She whispers "Well, I wouldn't want anybody to see us together." "Why not?" "Well, I wouldn't want anyone to know we are married." How would you feel? How do you think it makes God feel when we are embarrassed or ashamed to be seen with Him in public?

How do you think it makes Jesus feel when a homosexual "comes out of the closet" and declares to the world his or her sexual perversion, while many Christians are terrified to even mention the name of Jesus in public? God, help us!

I'll always remember a well-known couple in the ministry relating the story of having the opportunity to address a group of young Hindus about Christianity. Just before they were about to open the door to enter the room, the wife said to the husband, "I can't do it." He asked,

"Why not?" She said, "I'm scared!" He said, "What's to be afraid of, we're right!" She said, "Oh yes, that's right. Praise the Lord! Let's go!" If you know you're right, why be afraid?

Next, develop an eternal perspective. That is, to begin to interpret life Biblically. Here is a good place to start. Take your children to a junk yard. Show your son one of the cars on top of the pile and say to him, "You see that car, son? That was once a man's pride and joy. Most likely, the first man to own that car actually found his significance as a human being in that hunk of junk. Many of these men even stayed home from church on Sundays just to polish those things, and look at it now." I don't care if you drive a car worth $100,000. If you drive it every day, ten years from now it's going to be on a junk pile, and Jesus Christ will still be reigning in power and in glory unchanged.

When you get home from the junk yard, turn off the TV and turn on the Word of God. In an average lifetime, the Christian spends nine years of his life in front of the TV and only four months in church. Sadly, many never seriously study the Word of God from cover to cover. You don't have to be a rocket scientist to figure out that if you spend nine years in front of the TV compared to four months in church, and never seriously study the Word of God, intellectually, you will be closer to Archie Bunker and the Simpson's than Jesus Christ our Savior. I say that in love.

Is Jesus Christ, His work, His church, His kingdom, your number one passion in life? Is Jesus Christ your favorite thing to talk about and spend your money on? If you didn't know any more about your business or profession than you do about the Bible after the same number of years of exposure, where would you be in your business or profession today? Would you be bankrupt or fired? If it were against the law to be a Christian, and you were charged with being a Christian, would there be enough evidence to convict you in a court of law? Would your neighbors testify against you? Does anyone know you are a Christian, or are you the only one? Because, if you are the only person who knows it, there is a good chance you may not be one. Charles Haddon Spurgeon said, "If you do not have a passion to see people get saved, you can be sure you are not saved yourself." Ultimately, there is only one way to learn to trust the LORD. The answer is found in Proverbs 2:1-5:

> My son, if you will receive my sayings, and treasure my commandments within you, make your ear attentive to wisdom, incline your heart to understanding; for if you cry for discernment, lift your voice for understanding; if you seek her as silver, and search for her as for hidden treasures; then you will discern the fear of the LORD, and discover the knowledge of God.

When Martin Luther King Jr. was gaining momentum in his peaceful fight for civil rights in the 1960's, he was warned that if he did not stop, he would be assassinated. In one of the greatest speeches of his life, he said, "I have a dream that someday little black boys and little white boys will be able to play together." He said, "I have a dream, and I fear no man, for mine eyes have seen the glory of the coming of the Lord!" Not long after that, he was shot and killed by an assassin's bullet. He was dead before he hit the ground. I believe another thing happened before he hit the ground. I believe he was standing in the presence of Almighty God. And, if he was a Christian, the Lord said, "Well done, thou good and faithful servant. For you did not live for the praise of men, but for the praise that comes from the only God. You were faithful in a few things; enter into the joy of your Master!"

IN CLOSING

Friend, you may only have one chance to witness to the person with whom you are sharing, and his or her eternal destiny is hanging in the balance. Everything we say and do must be done for the glory of God. We are accountable to God for every word that we speak (Matt. 12:36), and teachers will be judged by an even stricter standard (James 3:1). What's at stake is where this person is going to spend eternity. Will there be blood on your hands when you stand before God, because you failed to heed the admonition of the LORD on how to present the Gospel? (see Ezek. 33:8,9, Acts 20:26)

You ignore this doctrine at your own risk. Over and over again the LORD speaks of demanding a return on His investment. The investment was the blood of His own Son on the cross! Apart from the Law, the cross makes no sense. He died in our place because we violated the Law.

God has entrusted you, Christian, with the secrets and the mysteries of the universe, and He will demand an accounting of how you handled His Word. How will you answer if on judgment day God asks (in effect), "What did you do with My Word? Were you faithful? I gave you all the tools you needed to present the gospel with power and authority. Did you use it? Where is your fruit?"

I have seen it time and time again. So many Christians, when they see a verse that is difficult or may cost them something to obey, say to themselves, "I'm not sure that's what it means," and just blow it off. Those who refuse to go wherever the Bible takes them never figure out why there is such a great gulf between the first century church and their own experience.

"But you, be sober in all things, endure hardship, do the work of an evangelist, fulfill your ministry." 2 Tim. 4:5 "And the things which you have heard from me in the presence of many witnesses, these entrust to faithful men, who will be able to teach others also." 2 Tim. 2:2

> For truly I say to you, until heaven and earth pass away, not the smallest letter or stroke shall pass away from the Law, until all is accomplished.
>
> Whoever then annuls one of the least of these commandments, and so teaches others, shall be called least in the kingdom of heaven; but whoever keeps and teaches {them}, he shall be called great in the kingdom of heaven. Matt 5:18-19

May the grace of our Lord Jesus Christ be with you!

SMALL GROUP DISCUSSION
QUESTIONS FOR CHAPTER TEN.

1. Jesus said, "If you are ashamed of me before men I will be ashamed of you before My father in Heaven." How does this verse make you feel? Why are so many people afraid of speaking up for Christ?

2. Why did Jesus send His disciples out in twos?

3. What was most meaningful to you in this chapter? Why?

4. What is the lesson for you personally in this chapter?

5. What is idolatry?

6. What are the main idols in our nation?

7. Share a time when you wanted to speak up for Christ but did not. Why didn't you?

8. Share a time when you did speak up for Jesus. How did it make you feel?

9. How do we get delivered from the fear of man?

10. What does God want you to do that you are not doing?

*Find a partner to pray with, and to hold you accountable for sharing the gospel on a regular basis.

BUT WE'RE NOT UNDER LAW, WE'RE UNDER GRACE!

Unfortunately, for many people, if you just mention the word "law," they go into spiritual shock. This condition is known to theologians as hyperdispensationalism." Their immediate response is to recite Romans 6:14, completely out of context!

> But we're not under Law, we're under Grace.

For those who might not understand the implications of taking a verse out of context, please refer back to chapter two. As for the verse at hand, first of all, the context of the entire chapter of Romans 6 is about dying to sin (breaking the Law), *not* grace nullifying the Law.

Whenever I hear that verse taken out of context, I like to ask, "Where does it say that in the Bible?" Almost always the response is something like, "I don't know, but it's in there somewhere." Then I ask, "Well, what Law is the Bible referring to? Is it the Law of God, the Law of Moses, the Pentateuch (the first five books of the Bible), the entire Old Testament, the civil law, the ceremonial Law, the moral Law, the letter of the Law, the spirit of the Law, the dispensation of Law, the Law of condemnation and death written on tablets of stone, the perfect Law of liberty, or the Law of Christ?" This is enough for most people to realize they do not understand the many facets of Law in the Bible, which accounts for all of the confusion. Many people mistakenly believe that because the New Testament says "Christ fulfilled the Law" that all Law is obsolete, and has no bearing on the life of a "New Testament Christian."

Let's take a close look at one of the most frequently abused verses in all the Bible, in its entirety.

> For sin shall not be master over you: for you are not under the Law, but under grace. Romans 6:14

Can Paul mean, after all he has just said in chapter 6 about giving up sin, which is breaking the Law (1 Jn. 3:4), that grace somehow nullifies the Law? In light of Romans 3:31, that is an impossible argument:

> Do we then nullify the Law through faith? May it never be! On the contrary, we establish the Law.

How is it possible to believe that we are no longer under any obligation to obey God's moral Law, since it is the Law that defines what sin is (Rom. 7:7, 1 Jn. 3:4)?

> What shall we say then? Is the Law sin? May it never be! On the contrary, I would not have come to know sin except through the Law; for I would not have known about coveting if the Law had not said, "You shall not covet."

To quote the second half of Romans 6:14 in an attempt to prove that the Law is no longer relevant is to turn the verse around 180 degrees and make it say the exact opposite of what it means. It's not obeying the (moral) Law that is forbidden, it's *breaking* the Law that we are supposed to give up! Look at the next two verses:

> What then? Shall we sin (transgress the Law) because we are not under Law but under grace? May it never be. Do you not know that when you present yourselves to someone {as} slaves for obedience, you are slaves of the one whom you obey, either of sin resulting in death, or of *obedience* resulting in righteousness?

OBEDIENCE TO WHAT?

If you are a Christian, the word "slave" in verse 16 is your job title, and the word "obedience" is your job description. The question is, obedience to what? This verse is perfectly clear. You are either a slave to sin, or you are a slave to righteousness!

Apparently, many people now think that since Jesus died on the cross it's okay for Christians to worship other gods or to bow down to statues. What about cursing using God's name? How many think God will just look the other way if we commit murder? Does anyone in his right New Testament mind think God will just smile and wink if Christians decide it's alright to commit adultery, or to marry more than one wife? What about stealing and lying? Are these transgressions now on the approved list since Christ made a way for us? Any takers for coveting against our neighbor? If anything, the New Testament *raised* the standard. The Old Testament said, "Thou shalt not commit adultery," but the New Testament says, "If you even look upon a woman to lust after her, you have committed adultery already in your heart" (Matt. 5:27-28)!

IF YOU'RE STILL NOT SURE, LET'S LOOK AT IT FROM ANOTHER POINT OF VIEW — WHAT IS THE MINISTRY OF GRACE!

The word "grace" in the Greek means not only unmerited favor, but, according to Spiros Zodhiates in the *Complete Word Study Dictionary of the New Testament*, grace "is initially regeneration, the work of the Holy Spirit in which spiritual life is given to man, and by which his nature is brought under the dominion of righteousness."[1] Now let's look at Titus 2:11–12:

> For the grace of God has appeared, bringing salvation [i.e., deliverance] to all men, instructing us to deny ungodliness and worldly desires and to live sensibly, righteously and godly in the present age, looking for the blessed hope and the appearing of the glory of our great God and Savior, Christ Jesus; who gave Himself for us, that He might redeem us from *every lawless deed* and purify for Himself a people for His own possession, zealous for good deeds. (emphasis mine)

LOOK AT WHAT PAUL SAYS IN THE VERY NEXT CHAPTER OF ROMANS

> Therefore the Law is holy, and the commandment is holy and just and good. Romans 7:12

Why would Paul use the present-tense verb *is* if the Law did not have spiritual relevance to his readers? Does Paul say the Law *was* holy, the commandment *was* holy, the Law *was* just and good?

FOR WE KNOW THAT THE
LAW IS SPIRITUAL
Romans 7:14

The understanding of what is meant by "the Law is spiritual" is defined for us by Jesus in Matthew 5. Jesus equates the physical act of murder (the letter of the Law) with unforgiveness, which is the spirit of the Law. Jesus equates adultery (the letter) with lust (the spiritual). The letter is objective, and the spirit is subjective. The physical can be seen by men, but the spiritual is a condition of the heart, which only God can see (1 Sam. 16:7). So, how do we correctly interpret verses like . . .

FOR CHRIST IS THE END OF THE LAW
FOR RIGHTEOUSNESS
TO EVERYONE WHO BELIEVES.
Romans 10:4

Please remember, most of the New Testament was originally written in Greek, not English. The word *end* could have been just as accurately translated as *aim* or *goal*. This is found in the margins of many study Bibles. Christ is the goal of the Law. For all practical purposes, virtually everything in the Old Testament pointed to Jesus. This does not mean, however, that we are now exempt from obedience to God's moral Law. On the contrary, holy obedience is the highest form of worship!

> I urge you therefore, brethren, by the mercies of God, to present your bodies a living and holy sacrifice, acceptable to God, {which is} your spiritual service of worship.
> Romans 12:1

If you get a speeding ticket and I pay the fine for you (like Jesus did for us), does that give you the right to go out and speed again? God forbid! The Lord's desire has always been for His people to walk in holy obedience.

FOR THROUGH THE LAW I DIED TO THE LAW, THAT I MIGHT LIVE TO GOD . . . . Galatians 2:19

It was the Law that showed Paul he could never be saved by keeping the Law! He died to the idea of trying to be *saved* by obeying it. The Law showed him he was a sinner, and that he needed God's grace. That is the most valuable and precious truth any human being could ever know (Gal. 3:24)!

YOU HAVE BEEN SEVERED FROM CHRIST, YOU WHO ARE SEEKING TO BE JUSTIFIED BY THE LAW; YOU HAVE FALLEN FROM GRACE.
Galatians 5:4

When a person seeks to be justified (saved) by keeping the Law, it is that very Law that will condemn him. For the Christian, the Ten Commandments represent practical holiness—*not* justification by works! For the non-Christian, that same Law is his death sentence. You are either under Law, or you are under grace. I love what the late Dr. Walter Martin said when speaking of those who reject God's gift of grace through Jesus: "If they don't want Jesus, be sure and leave 'em with Moses!"

DO WE THEN MAKE VOID THE LAW THROUGH FAITH? CERTAINLY NOT! ON THE CONTRARY, WE ESTABLISH THE LAW.
Romans 3:31

We are saved by grace alone, through faith alone, through Christ alone, plus nothing. Our salvation is based on the fact that Christ satisfied the demands of the Law on our behalf. There is nothing in the course of mankind's history, nothing in the universe that so established, upheld, or confirmed the validity of the Law as when the wrath of God was poured out on the sinless Lamb of God on the cross of Calvary. But, its work continues. Since the beginning of time, every man, woman, and child that has ever been born has died (with the exception of Enoch and Elijah), death (with the exception of Jesus) is the result of sin, and "sin is the transgression of the Law" (1 Jn. 3:4).

Every time someone dies, their death proves that the Law is still in effect and still being enforced. The Law says that if you sin, you shall surely die (see Rom. 6:23; Gen. 2:17). Just as death presupposes life, so grace presupposes Law.

FOR THE LAW OF THE SPIRIT OF LIFE IN CHRIST JESUS HAS SET YOU FREE FROM THE LAW OF SIN AND DEATH
Romans 8:2

Let me answer this one with a question . . .

HOW CAN THE TEN COMMANDMENTS BE REFERRED TO AS "THE LAW OF SIN AND DEATH" IN 2 CORINTHIANS 3:9, ALSO BE CALLED "THE PERFECT LAW OF LIBERTY" IN JAMES 1:25 AND 2:10?

The Law of sin and death in 2 Corinthians 3 is also the perfect Law of liberty in James 2. It all depends on which side of the cross you're on. The same Law that once condemned me (before I was a Christian), now points me to holiness. This verse (Rom. 8:2), sets me free from the condemnation of the Law, not my obligation, based on love, to obey it!

> . . . that law, so terrible to the sinner, is a law of liberty to the regenerated one, because it commands the very behavior in which the one born of God finds his joy and delight.[2]

APPENDIX TWO

SATAN'S MASTER PLAN OF EVANGELISM, AND THE IMMORAL MAJORITY

The number one deception in our world is the same lie that Satan used with Adam and Eve when he said, "You surely shall not die" (i.e., be separated from God). Many, if not most, of the people I witness to are deceived into thinking that God will not reject them because they are basically "good people." After all, they reason, "I'm a good person; I've never murdered anyone." The problem with that line of "reasoning" is that we humans are not the ones who define what "good" is. Scripture says, "Only God is good" (Matt. 19:17). God alone is perfect, and is therefore the only One qualified and capable of establishing and enforcing an absolute, universal standard of righteousness and truth for all people.

"GOING TO CHURCH DOESN'T MAKE YOU A CHRISTIAN, ANY MORE THAN EATING AT McDONALD'S MAKES YOU A HAMBURGER."[1]

Sadly, there are many people who think they are Christians simply because they "believe in God" and go to church. Since many people who attend church regularly do not study their Bibles firsthand, they end up getting their "daily bread" only once a week. To compound the problem, many of these weekly feedings are served by pastors who, by and large, are not serious students of the Bible themselves! Consequently, the stuff they serve is often stale, secondhand, and boring. It's one thing to read the Bible and come up with a few "appropriate comments" for Sunday morning, it's another thing to seriously study the Word of God in order to live and teach with results. It's one thing to come up with something to say because you are having a meeting, it's quite another to have a meeting because you have something to say.

For the worldly minded, or liberal minister, there is little or no incentive to preach the whole counsel of God, since to do so could be offensive. This could hurt church attendance, which means giving would decline, which could cost the pastor his job. This is why so much of the church looks more like a social club on a cruise ship, rather than a battleship, armed and ready to storm the gates of hell. The attitude of many church goers (and preachers) is that *it's okay to have church on Sunday, as long as it doesn't interfere with lunch or the game.* The end product is a church that is, for the most part, indistinguishable from the world. The word church (Ekklesia), means: An assembly of God's people, *called out from the world.*

GEORGE GALLUP

"Most Americans who profess Christianity don't know the basic teachings of the faith, and they don't act significantly different from non-Christians in their daily lives. Over all, the Sunday school and religious education system in this country is not working. Not being grounded in the faith, these professing believers are open for anything that comes along. Studies show that new age beliefs for example, are just as strong among traditionally religious people as among those who are not traditionally religious. And the churched are just as likely as the unchurched to engage in unethical behavior. The studies also show a growing percentage of Christians believe they can sustain their faith without going to church."[2]

I recently heard a former Jehovah's (False) Witness on the radio explain how he knocked on doors for six years, and not once in all that time did he meet a Christian who could refute his "errors" using a Bible!

I heard a missionary relate that in Africa there is a group of people who have a legalistic understanding of Christianity. He almost seemed to be bragging as he said, "Some of our people have been stoned for preaching grace." Yet they continue to preach grace! When a man thinks he can be saved by "being good enough," you don't just keep preaching grace. His problem is, he doesn't understand the Law (Rom. 3:20). For God to overlook even one sin would make Him unjust!

If you are caught going twenty-five miles over the speed limit by the radar gun of a policeman, will it help your case if you suggest to the policeman that you will be more than happy to go twenty-five miles under the speed limit to make up for it? After all, you're a good person, right? That's what they all say. Once the law has been broken, there is nothing you can do to change it. The righteous demands of the law must be satisfied. All you can do at this point is to pay the fine. True justice demands that the appropriate penalty be paid for just one infraction. Would you want to live in a society where lawbreakers were simply excused for their crimes without justice being served?

I have actually heard Christian leaders say things like, "There are no laws in the New Testament." Friend, you can't even play Tidily Winks without rules! It is no coincidence that the longest chapter in the Bible (Psalm 119) is about loving God's Law. Does this sound like a man in bondage to you?

> So I will keep Thy law continually, forever and ever. And I will walk at liberty, for I seek Thy precepts. I will also speak of Thy testimonies before kings, and shall not be shamed. And I shall delight in Thy commandments, which I love. And I shall lift up my hands to Thy commandments, which I love; and I will meditate on Thy statutes. Ps. 119:44-48

EXCUSES, EXCUSES!

Ever since the garden of Eden, man has gone to great lengths to avoid, deny, ignore, suppress, or redefine the doctrine of sin. One artful dodge is to call it crime. In this case, we are no longer breaking God's Law, but man's. This shifts the responsibility from the church to the state. Today we refer to alcoholism and drug addition as a disease rather than a moral weakness. You can't repent of a disease. Homosexuality (an abomination to God) is now called a "preexisting genetic condition." Nothing to be sorry for here, it's perfectly natural, right? Wrong! Otherwise, God would have been unjust in destroying Sodom and Gomorrah. (See Genesis 19, Lev. 18:22, 1 Cor. 6:9-10, Gal. 5:19-21, Rev. 21:8.) There seems to be no end to man's shell-game with words. Today we have no fault divorce, and no-fault insurance. We blame everybody and everything except the real culprit. When God confronted Adam about his transgression in the Garden of Eden, Adam turned right around and said, "It was the woman you gave me."

RUNNING TO WIN

As a child I loved to run. All the way through school I never lost a running race. Every year in school when they posted the names and the times for the 50-yard dash, I was #1. Even at my dad's company picnics I won every race, every year. When I was in 8th grade, however, I ran into a little technical problem. When it came time to run the dash that year my name was called, I came up to the line, the gun went off, the clock started, and I took off like lightning. About halfway through the race, however, the 8th grade girls' class came filing out behind me. It seems a couple of them yelled out, "Go! Go!" and I made the mistake of looking back to see who it was. That look cost me two seconds! As soon as the coach told me my time, I said, "Coach, you saw what happened. You know I can do better than that. Please let me run it again." His "No" was final. I was posted in second place that year!

Fact: The shortest distance between two points is a straight line. If you even look to the right or to the left, not only will it cost you; you may even lose the race! Remember Lot's wife? If you want to run the race of evangelism to win souls, do not look to the right or to the left. The moral Law is the straightest line and the shortest distance to the Gospel you will ever find (Gal. 3:24).

NOTES

Chapter 1: The Most Awesome Demonstration of Power the World has Ever Seen

1. The Video, *Discovering the Real Mt. Sinai* is available from the BASE Institute, Palmer Lake, CO.

2. Hebert Lockyer, *All the Miracles of the Bible* (Grand Rapids: Zondervon Books, 1961), 70.

3. Lockyer.

4. Frederica Mathewes-Green, in an article by *Christianity Today* magazine.

Chapter 2: Something Old Something New Something Bold Something True

1. Michael Horton, *The Law of Perfect Freedom* (Chicago: Moody Press, 1993), 28.

2. Sidney Greidanus, *Preaching Christ from the Old Testament* (Grand Rapids: Eerdmans Publishing Co., 1999).

3. Archibald Naismith, *2400 Outlines, Notes, Quotes, and Anecdotes for Sermons* (Grand Rapids: Baker Books, reprinted 1991), 79.

Chapter 3: The Law of God, Written on Every Man's Heart

1. From an article entitled: *"Confessions of a Professed Atheist,"* Report: Perspective on the News, Vol. 3 (June 1966), p.19. From an article by Helming, *"An Interview with God."*

2. A live interview with Lee Strobel on *Midday Connection.* WMBI FM Radio, in Chicago. 11/29/2000

3. I am indebted to Lakita Garth for this excellent illustration on purity.

Chapter 4: What's Wrong with the Modern Gospel?

1. James Montgomery Boice, *The Minor Prophets* *(Grand Rapids:* Kregal Publications, 1983, 1996), 49.

2. J. C. Ryle, *Holiness* (Darlington: Evangelical Press, first pub. 1879, 1995), 1.

3. Keith Green, *What's Wrong with the Modern Gospel* (Lindale: Last Days Ministries, 1981).

4. Ravi Zacharias, *Let My People Think* (radio program).

Chapter 5: Jesus Christ the Master Evangelist

1. Warren Wiersbe, *The Bible Exposition Commentary* (Wheaton: Victor Books, 1989).

2. Ibid., 72.

3. Ibid., 250.

4. A.C. Gaebelein, *The Gospel of Matthew* (New York: Our Hope, 1910), 104.

5. Arthur W. Pink, *Exposition of the Gospel of John* (Grand Rapids: Zondervan, 1975), 106.

6. Leon Morris, *The Gospel According to John* (Grand Rapids: William B. Eerdmans, 1995), 295.

7. Matthew Henry, *The Bethany Parallel Commentary New Testament* (Minneapolis: Bethany House, 1983), 453.

Chapter 6: Don't Take My Word for It

1. C.H. Spurgeon, *Lectures to My Students* (Grand Rapids: Zondervan, 1954), 338.

2. John Calvin, *Institutes of the Christian Religion.*

3. John Wesley, *The Works of John Wesley, vols. 5–6* (Grand Rapids: Baker Books, 1991), 449.

4. Comfort (Video). *The Ten Cannons of God's Law* (Living Waters Publications Bellflower, CA)

5. Comfort (Video).

6. Henry, Ibid.

7. Comfort (Video).

8. Comfort (Video).

9. Augustine.

10. Jonathan Edwards, John MacArthur Jr., *The Vanishing Conscience* (Dallas: Word, 1994), 245.

11. Spurgeon.

12. Wesley, 445.

13. Comfort, 82.

14. Comfort, *Life, Liberty, and the Pursuit of Righteous* (Bellflower: Living Waters, 1997).

15. Arthur W. Pink, *The Ten Commandments* (Grand Rapids: Baker Books, 1976), 14.

16. H. A. Ironside, *Hebrews, James, Peter* (Neptune: Loizeaux Brothers, Inc., 1947, 82), 21.

17. Morris.

18. Walter Kaiser, *Toward an Exegetical Theology (Grand Rapids: Baker* Books, 1981).

19. John MacArthur, *The Gospel According to Jesus* (Grand Rapids: Zondervan, 1988), 84.

20. Horton, 36.

21. Kay Arthur, *Beloved*, July 20th.

22. Alexander Maclaren, *Expositions of Holy Scripture* (Grand Rapids: Baker Books, 1974),

23. Donald Grey Barnhouse, *Romans, Vol. I* (Grand Rapids: Eerdmans, 1952), 275.

24. William Barclay on James 1:25, 2:10.

25. Jamieson, Fausset, Brown, *The Bethany Parallel Commentary on the New Testament* (Minneapolis: Bethany House, 1983), 898.

26. D. Martyn Lloyd-Jones, *Romans, Atonement & Justification* (Grand Rapids: Zondervan, 1989), 21.

27. Maclaren, 98.

28. Gleason Archer, *A Survey of Old Testament Introduction* (Chicago: Moody Press, 1964), 253.

29. R.C. Sproul, [audio tape], used by permission.

30. Erwin Lutzer.

31. D.A. Carson, [Lecture in seminary class at Trinity International University], used by permission.

32. Erwin Lutzer, This was a personal interview at Moody Memorial Church in Chicago. I asked Dr. Lutzer to critique my tract on evangelism using the Ten Commandments, followed by an illustration of grace. His answer was classic.

Chapter 7: Presenting the Gospel in the Power of the Spirit

1. Comfort, [videotape].

Chapter 8: The Perfect Law of Liberty

1. William Barclay, *The Letters of James and Peter* (Philadelphia: Westminster Press, 1976), 60.

2. Thanks to Matthew J. Slick of the Christian Apologetics and Research Ministry.

3. Ravi Zacharias, *Let My People Think* (radio program).

4. Ironside.

Chapter 10: The Fear of Man vs. The Fear of God

1. A.W. Tozer, *The Best of A.W. Tozer* (Grand Rapids: Baker Books, 1978), 177.

2. A.W. Tozer *The Knowledge of the Holy* (New York, NY: Harper Collins, 1961,) 1.

Appendix One: But We're Not Under Law, We're Under Grace

1. Spiros Zodhiates, *Complete Word Study Dictionary: New Testament* (Chattanooga: AMG, 1993), 1469.

2. Ironside.

Appendix Two: Satan's Master Plan of Evangelism and the Immoral Majority

1. Keith Green.

2. Quoted in , *National and International Religion Report Vol. 5 No.11* (Washington D.C.: Media Management, 1991), 1.